ACKNOWLEDGMENTS

A special thanks to all those who have contributed to my knowledge and brought this book together. My parents, for teaching and encouraging me to appreciate craft alcohol instead of abusing it. My sister Charlie, who introduced me to the hospitality industry. Sam and Josh, who taught me so much foundational knowledge about the world of mixology and spirits. Fleur, for designing and creating the book and brand. Madison, for her writing and editing.

A huge thank you to Matt and Steve for all their hard work, passion, and knowledge that helped bring the book together.

And of course, to Mike, for encouraging me to create the book and bringing it to life!

_____

Authors: George Grbich and Madison Fisher
Design: Fleur Curac
Website: worldginguides.com
Instagram: @nzginguide
Facebook: Guide to New Zealand Gin

_____

PUBLISHED BY
People Media Group
Newmarket, Auckland
peoplemediagroup.co.nz

_____

© People Media Group 2022
ISBN: 978-0-473-64655-4

CONTENTS

7	The Team	38	Herrick Creek Moose Lake
8	Styles of Gin	39	Pink Grapefruit & Kawakawa Gin
9	New Zealand Native Botanicals	40	Sauvignon Blanc & Green Tea Gin
		41	Wild Ginseng & Manuka Honey Gin
10	**CLASSIC**		
12	1919 Classic	42	Humdinger Citrus Gin
13	Butterfly Effect Gin	43	Humdinger Dry Gin
14	Batch10 New Zealand Dry	44	imagination Reikorangi Dry
15	Black Collar Gin	45	Juno Emily
16	Weekender Original Dry	46	Juno Extra Fine
17	Broken Heart Angel Share Gin	47	Juno Jean
18	Broken Heart Gin	48	Juno Monica
19	Broken Heart Queenstown Gin	49	Monica Gin
20	The Source	50	Juno Summer 2022
21	Chemistry Gin	51	1963 Citrus
22	Curiosity Classic	52	Championz
23	Curious Dry	53	Delightful Dry
24	Dancing Sands Dry	54	Gin & Bare It: Original
25	Our Coast	55	Laughing Club Gin
26	Te Aro Dry	56	Lighthouse Original
27	duo Citrine	57	LTD Issue No.1
28	duo Heliodor	58	Racketeer London Dry
29	duo Moonstone	59	NDC Art Deco Gin
30	Elsewhere Gin - North Canterbury	60	NDC New Zealand Dry Gin
		61	No8 Dunners Dry
31	Exhibit A No.580	62	Whanganui Dry Gin
32	Forth Luck Premium Gin	63	Papaka Road Gin
33	Forth Luck NZ Dry Gin	64	Pink & White - White Dry Gin
34	Good George Aotearoa Dry Gin	65	Pollen Gin
35	Good George Lemon Gin	66	Reid + Reid Native Gin
36	For Fucks Sake 2021	67	Reid + Reid Rev. Dawson
37	What's Fucking Next 2022	68	Rifters Original

69	Roots Marlborough Dry Gin	103	Dr Beak Premium Gin
70	Lovers Leap Gin	104	Dunedin Dry Gin
71	Scapegrace Classic	105	The Bay Gin
72	Uncommon Central Otago Early Harvest	106	Elsewhere Gin - Endevour Inlet
73	Uncommon Hawkes Bay Late Harvest	107	Elsewhere Gin - Hahei
		108	Elsewhere Gin - Little River
74	Black Robin Rare Dry Gin	109	Elsewhere X Austin Club Little Akaloa Gin
75	Sir Winston Dry	110	1564 Venus & Adonis Shakespare's Gin
76	Solace London Dry		
77	Taupo Distilling 5 Mile Gin	111	The Artist
78	Twelfth Hour Gin	112	The Beast with Two Backs
79	Vicars Son Classic London Dry	113	The Novelist
80	Vicars Son Accesion	114	The Poet
81	Vicars Son Revalation	115	The Vintner
82	Vicars Son The Holy Spirit	116	Parma Violet
83	Vicars Son Without Sin	117	Signature Citrus
84	Victor Gin Heavy Botanical	118	Albertine
85	Waiheke Distilling London Dry	119	Autumn Gin
86	Washhouse Gin	120	Blossom Parade
87	YEN Gin	121	East Block 200
		122	Hector's Long Harbour Ocean Wash
88	**CONTEMPORARY**		
90	Ariki Ultra Premium Gin	123	Wakame Seaweed
91	Awildian Coromandel Dry	124	Island Original
92	Awildian Coromandel Dry - Blue Edition	125	Juniper Jinn
		126	Juno Autumn 2022
93	Awildian Coromandel Spiced Gin	127	Juno Winter 2022
		128	Agathas Tears Dark Gin
94	The Bureaucrat	129	Eliza's Claim Dry Gin
95	The Doyenne	130	Eliza's Claim Gold Gin
96	Knockleveigh Cambridge Dry Gin	131	Sirius' Find Truffle Gin
97	Curious Recipe #23	132	Kakapo Kawakawa and Pink Peppercorn
98	Coatsvillien Spice Gin 2022 Harvest		
		133	Kakapo Manuka Honey and Elderflower
99	Distillers Proof Tea Tree		
100	Smoke & Embers	134	Katipo Aotearoa Dry Gin
101	Dr Beak Garden Gin	135	1963 Butterfly Pea Flower
102	Dr Beak Yuzu Garden Gin	136	Greenstone Gin

137	Koakoa Tini Remana Gin	168	Scapegrace Black
138	The Bond Store Kawakawa Gin	169	Storm Black Wolf Gin
139	Lady H Gin	170	Strange Nature
140	Gin & Bare It: Optical Illusion	171	Victor Gin Lime Leaf
141	Lavender Infused	172	Spirit of Waiheke
142	Saffron Infused	173	Wild Diamond Black Gin
143	Racketeer Spiced Gin	174	Wild Diamond Original

139	Lady H Gin
140	Gin & Bare It: Optical Illusion
141	Lavender Infused
142	Saffron Infused
143	Racketeer Spiced Gin
144	Racketeer Verbena Gin
145	Peninsula Gin
146	Shearwater Gin
147	Woolshed Gin
148	NDC Adorn
149	NDC Hemp Gin
150	NDC Meow Lucky Gin
151	NDC NZ Native Gin
152	NDC Verdigris
153	No8 Hibiscus Gin
154	No8 Horopito Gin
155	Papaiti Gin Orchard
156	Sundown Dry
157	Little Biddy Gin - Classic
158	Little Biddy Gin - Snow
159	Reid + Reid Zesty Lemon Gin
160	Rifters Quartz
161	1743 Riot
162	1920 Rose
163	Ruin - The Courage
164	Ruin -The Valley
165	Sandymount Chapter 1
166	Sandymount Chapter 2
167	Sandymount Tekouka Forrest Gin

176	**NAVY STRENGTH**
178	Broken Heart Navy
179	Dancing Sands Wasabi Gin
180	Nine Fathoms Canterbury Gin
181	Island Navy
182	Lighthouse Hawthorn
183	NDC Old Navy
184	Roots Norwester Navy Strength Gin
185	Scapegrace Gold
186	Vicars Son Holy Spirit
188	**PINK**
190	1919 Pink
191	Batch10 Pink
192	Juno Spring 2022
193	Laughing Club Pink Gin
194	Pink & White - Pink Dry
195	Little Biddy Gin - Pink
196	**FLAVOURED**
198	1919 Pineapple Bits
199	Hector's French Farm Petit Pinot Gin
200	Blush Boysenberry
201	Blush Rhubarb
202	Blush Summer Citrus
203	Weekender Lemon Gin
204	Weekender Orange Gin
205	Weekender Peach Gin
206	Angel's Share Collectors Edition

207	Bella - Wild Plum Gin Elixir	243	Rhubarb Gin
208	Broken Heart Pinot Noir	244	Sheep Milk & Honey
209	Broken Heart Quince	245	Wild Diamond Feijoa Gin
210	Broken Heart Rhubarb	246	Wild Diamond Saffron Gin
211	Bureaucrats: Black Doris Plum	247	Wild Diamond Vanilla Gin
212	Curious Pinot Barrel Sloe	**248**	**AGED**
213	Curious Ruby	250	Awildian Manuka Gin
214	Dancing Sands Sauvignon Blanc	251	Broken Heart Barrel Aged Gin
215	Dancing Sands Sun-Kissed	252	Curiosity Gin - Negroni Special
216	Elsewhere - Central Otago		
217	Chic Gin	253	Dancing Sands Barrel Aged Gin
218	Good George Doris Plum	254	Elsewhere - Fox River
219	Posy Pink Gin Liqueur	255	The Pioneer
220	Humdinger Sloe Gin	256	I.F. (Ignis Fatuus) Gin)
221	Damson Plum	257	Humdinger Bourbon Barrel Aged Gin
222	Lewis Farm Strawberry Gin		
223	Rhubarb & Raspberry	258	Black Barn Syrah Barrel Aged Gin
224	Juniper Jinn Liqueur		
225	Rose Jinn Liqueur	259	Styx Barrel-Aged Gin
226	Trader Jinn Liqueur	260	Gin & Bare It Ginisky
227	Ruby Gin	261	Lighthouse Barrel Aged Gin
228	Lavender Hill Sloe Gin	262	Woodcutter Barrel Aged Gin
229	Lavender Hill Smoked Honey Gin	263	Washhouse Barrel Aged Gin
230	The Racketeer Blackcurrant	**264**	**ALCOHOL FREE SPIRIT**
231	The Racketeer Plum	266	Broken Heart 0% Spirit
232	NDC Adorn Rose	267	Ecology & Co. Asian Spice
233	No8 Moka Gin	268	Ecology & Co. London Dry
234	Rose & Twig Blood Orange		
235	Rose & Twig Blueberry	**270**	**FEVER-TREE**
236	Rose & Twig Pomegranate	271	A Short History on Tonic
237	Sundown Black Doris Gin	272	The Perfect Gin & Tonic
238	Sundown Grapefruit & Elderflower Gin	274	Tonics
		276	Gingers & Cola
239	Little Biddy Gin - Hazy	277	Sodas
240	Solace Raspbery & Cranberry		
241	Victor Blanc de Blanc	**278**	**DISTILLERY DIRECTORY**
242	Red Ruby Gin		

TASTERS' PICKS

Our tasters have selected an 'Ultimate Mix' for a range of Classic Gin Cocktails

Our tasters have selected an 'Ultimate Mix' for a range of Fever-Tree Mixers

Our tasters have selected a Top Pick in each category. Look out for this badge.

Our tasters have selected a range of Highly Commended gins from each section.

Our 2021 tasters selected a top pick, and a range or highly commended gins from each category.

Our 2020 tasters selected a top pick from each category

THE TEAM

GEORGE GRBICH - TASTER & AUTHOR
George is a New Zealand based spirits writer and judge with many years of experience working in the hospitality industry. A passionate gin advocate whose love for spirits sprung from his father's love for a good gin and tonic. He has extensive knowledge of the New Zealand and Australian Gin industries, comprehensively tasting just under 1000 Australasian gins over the past two years. Deeply intrigued by the variety of styles and distillation techniques being used in the modern world of gin, he is a strong supporter of the ever growing boutique and artisanal spirits scene. He has also obtained the WSET Level 2 Award in Spirits qualification in 2021.

MATT BRIDGE - TASTER
Matt is the founder and distiller of Lunatic & Lover Distillery, which opened its doors in Auckland in 2019. Although principally making rum, he is no stranger to the peculiarities of botanicals as their flagship rums are flavoured with a variety of distilled botanicals. He also consults on various gin projects and recipe development and when pushed, will admit to enjoying a good G&T almost as much as rum. Whilst enthusiastic about distilled spirits in general, he has a particular passion for the intricacies of spirits production and can often be found buried in an obscure research paper. He holds professional qualifications from both the Institute of Brewing and Distilling and WSET, and sits on the Distilled Spirits Aotearoa committee.

STEVE BENNETT MW - TASTER
Steve Bennett, Master of Wine, has more than 30 years of experience working in the retail, importation, distribution, production, and educational sectors of the liquor industry. In 1994 he became the youngest ever of only 450 people to have passed the Master of Wine Examination. Steve has educated both consumers and liquor industry professionals in NZ, Australia, the US, UK, and Europe. As well as a strong professional interest in wine, Steve has a personal passion for beer and gin which he has tasted widely during his international travels.

STYLES OF GIN

Although there are many varying definitions of gin styles, here is our interpretation of what we believe best represents the New Zealand Gin category.

Classic Dry: Gins with a prominent juniper flavour that also incorporate traditional botanicals.

Modern Dry: Gins with a prominent juniper flavour that also incorporate modern, new world and/or local botanicals to enhance its flavour.

Contemporary: Gins with modern, new world and/or local botanical flavour that is more prominent than juniper.

Navy Strength: Gins bottled at 54.5% ABV (alcohol by volume) and above.

Pink: Distilled gins that have natural pink colouring due to the redistillation of berries, red fruits or pink botanicals.

Flavoured: Gins with additional flavour influence, often from fruits or flavourings post distillation through a variety of methods.

Gin Liqueur: Gins with the addition of sugar, sweetened over a certain volume post distillation.

Sloe: Distilled gins steeped post distillation in sloe berries and mixed with sugar.

Aged: Gin rested for a noted period of time. Generally influenced by wood, rested in a tank with staves or woodchips, or matured in a barrel or cask.

Alcohol-Free Spirit: Distilled without the presence of alcohol.

NEW ZEALAND BOTANICALS

Lacey Bourne, Horticulturist & Native Botanical Enthusiast

HOROPITO *(Pseudowintera Colorata)*
A small evergreen tree, often found on the edges of forests throughout New Zealand, with an abundance of volatile oils in its leaves. Traditionally used to help with oral health and as a painkiller, due to its natural astringent and antiseptic properties. The bioactive compound, polygodial, gives the foliage its distinct cayenne pepper punch, which builds and leaves a burning sensation in the mouth. This pepperiness transfers well through the distillation process and creates a warming spice in gin.

TARATA *(Pittosporum Eugenioides)*
A tree, also known as Lemonwood, commonly found in lowland and mountain forests throughout New Zealand that grows to 12-13m. It has pale, almost white bark, glossy light-green leaves, and strongly perfumed flowers with a sweet, honey-like scent. Its resin can be chewed as gum and the leaves, when crushed, smell like freshly cut lemon. When distilled, the leaves offer bright grassy citrus notes to the nose, with subtle pine resin, sweet floral tones, and citrus on the palate.

KAWAKAWA *(Macropiper Excelsum)*
A cousin of black pepper (Piper nigrum), this shrub has heart shaped leaves and berries arranged on spikes, which can both be distilled. The unripe fruit is often used, delivering a hint of bitterness reminiscent of cardamom, cloves, and ginger, along with rich dried stone fruit. While the leaves bring black pepper and a fresh flush on the palate. The desirable leaves are the ones with the holes made by the caterpillar of the Kawakawa Looper moth, as it prompts the plant to produce more active compounds in that area.

MĀNUKA *(Leptospermum Scoparium)*
A shrub or small tree, also known as Tea Tree, found throughout New Zealand that tolerates a wide range of growing conditions, including low-fertility soils. Predominantly, the small but oil- rich leaves are used, however, its bark, flowers, and honey are often used too. When distilled, the leaves are very aromatic, with lifted floral notes, layered with dried pimento spice. On the palate you will find pleasing eucalyptus scented resin, gentle mulled orchard fruits, and elegant earthy tones.

MOUNTAIN TOATOA *(Phyllocladus Alpinus)*
The smallest and most cold tolerant member of the Phyllocladus genus found in New Zealand, this tree is also known as Mountain Celery Pine. In the North Island, the common form of this tree is found southward from the Coromandel Peninsula, and in the South Island it is predominantly found on the West Coast. When distilled, it exhibits lively tannic characteristics, with opulent fresh pine resin notes and delicate citrus.

HARAKEKE, NEW ZEALAND FLAX *(Phormium Tenax)*
A flax that grows from coastal to subalpine altitudes throughout New Zealand. Many parts of the plant are edible, including the nectar of the flowers, the gum from the base of the leaves, and the seeds. However, it is the seeds that are most often used as a botanical. Found from late summer through to early autumn, they are rich in fatty acids and when distilled, deliver a nutty nuance.

CLASSIC

CLASSIC DRY

Gins with a prominent juniper flavour that also incorporate traditional botanicals.

MODERN DRY

Gins with a prominent juniper flavour that also incorporate modern, new world and/or local botanicals to enhance its flavour.

———————

1919 Classic Gin

41% ABV

A modern dry style gin, 1919 Classic Gin celebrates old world charm with botanicals like juniper, angelica root, and cinnamon in combination with Otago cherries, Manuka honey, and organic lemons and oranges.

– VOL. 3 –
HIGHLY COMMENDED
GUIDE TO NEW ZEALAND GIN

FEVER-TREE ULTIMATE MIX
GUIDE TO NEW ZEALAND GIN

– 2021 –
HIGHLY COMMENDED
GUIDE TO NEW ZEALAND GIN

DISTILLERY:
1919 Distilling, Auckland

BOTANICALS:
Juniper, Coriander Seed, Green Cardamom, Lemon Peel, Orange Peel, Angelica Root, Cherry, Mānuka Honey & Cinnamon

TASTING NOTES:
Aromatic green spice, dry citrus and tart cherry on the nose, initial juniper with tart cherry, earthy coriander and orange peel on the palate, drying spice and tart fruit to finish.

SERVING SUGGESTION:
Enjoy with Fever-Tree Aromatic Tonic Water.

Arrival Gin Butterfly Effect
43% ABV

A modern dry gin, Arrival Gin Butterfly Effect is a twist on their version of a New Zealand classic dry gin, using Butterfly Pea Flower as a botanical, which gives it an electric blue colour that turns pink when mixed with tonic water or lemon.

DISTILLERY:
Aurora Distillery, Lower Hutt

BOTANICALS:
Juniper, Coriander Seed, Angelica Root, Orris Root, Liquorice, Cassia, Orange Peel, Grapefruit Peel, Hibiscus, Kawakawa & Butterfly Pea Flower

TASTING NOTES:
Pleasant grapefruit with coriander and powdered cinnamon on the nose, pronounced orange and grapefruit with coriander on the palate, warming cassia and mellowing citrus to finish.

SERVING SUGGESTION:
Enjoy with Fever-Tree Premium Indian Tonic Water.

batch10 New Zealand Gin
40% ABV

A classic dry style gin with a New Zealand twist, batch10 New Zealand Gin is smooth and crisp with a distinct hint of citrus that honours the orchards of the nearby Omaha and Matakana areas.

DISTILLERY:
batch10 Spirits, Puhoi

BOTANICALS:
Juniper, Coriander Seed, Cassia, Angelica Root, Nutmeg, Citrus Peel, Tangerine, Orris Root, Star Anise, Anise, Lemon, Orange & Cardamom

TASTING NOTES:
Soft subtle spice with coriander on the nose, classic notes of light juniper, lemon peel and baking spice on the palate, spice mellows to finish.

SERVING SUGGESTION:
Enjoy with Fever-Tree Premium Indian Tonic Water.

Black Collar Gin
42% ABV

A modern dry style gin, Black Collar Gin is made traditionally by macerating their botanicals overnight before distillation with no vapour infusion, water baths, essences, or artificial flavourings.

DISTILLERY:
Black Collar Distillery, Kerikeri

BOTANICALS:
Juniper, Coriander Seed, Liquorice, Marshmallow & Others

TASTING NOTES:
Damp earthy forest floor with light nutty spice on the nose, pronounced liquorice and continuing spice on the palate, settling earthy tones to finish.

SERVING SUGGESTION:
Enjoy with Fever-Tree Mediterranean Tonic Water.

Weekender Classic Dry Gin

41% ABV

Weekender Classic Dry Gin was developed over the course of 12 months and designed to make an everyday gin and tonic, packed full of classic botanicals.

DISTILLERY:
Blush Gin Ltd., Auckland

BOTANICALS:
Juniper, Coriander Seed, Angelica Root, Orange Peel, Lemon Peel & Orris Root

TASTING NOTES:
Light coriander with angelica on the nose, sweet citrus notes with light juniper and coriander on the palate, hints of lemon lead a quick finish.

SERVING SUGGESTION:
Enjoy with Fever-Tree Refreshingly Light Indian Tonic Water.

Broken Heart Angel's Share Gin
40% ABV

A modern dry style gin, Broken Heart Angel's Share Batch No 01 is a collector's edition made in small batches and inspired by their original gin, playing on the frontiers of balance with its botanicals.

DISTILLERY:
Broken Heart Spirits,
Arrow Junction

BOTANICALS:
Juniper, Coriander Seed, Lavender, Angelica Root, Citrus, Orange Flower, Hops, Ginger, Pimento, Cinnamon, Thyme, Orange Peel & Hemp

TASTING NOTES:
Floral lavender and fragrant green herbs lead the nose, lemon sherbet with pepper spice and persistent juniper on the palate, bitter green herbs and lemon to finish.

SERVING SUGGESTION:
Enjoy with Fever-Tree Mediterranean Tonic Water.

Broken Heart Gin

40% ABV

A modern dry style gin, Broken Heart Gin balances earthy, floral, spicy, and fresh flavour profiles to capture the essence of a dry Central Otago summer.

DISTILLERY:
Broken Heart Spirits, Arrow Junction

BOTANICALS:
Juniper, Coriander Seed, Lavender, Angelica Root, Citrus, Orange Flower, Hops, Ginger, Pimento & Cinnamon

TASTING NOTES:
Juniper leads with an array of citrus on the nose, light juniper, sweet citrus and warming spice on the palate, hot peppercorn and dry spice to finish.

SERVING SUGGESTION:
Enjoy with Fever-Tree Mediterranean Tonic Water.

Broken Heart Queenstown Edition
40% ABV

A modern dry style gin, Broken Heart Queenstown Edition Gin was created in celebration of their 9th birthday by combining the botanical essences of their Navy Gin with the alcohol content of their Original Gin.

DISTILLERY:
Broken Heart Spirits, Arrow Junction

BOTANICALS:
Juniper, Coriander Seed, Lavender, Angelica Root, Citrus, Orange Flower, Hops, Ginger, Pimento & Cinnamon

TASTING NOTES:
Coriander, juniper and angelica lead a classic nose, pronounced citrus, green herbs and hints of pine on the palate, earthy coriander and lavender linger to finish.

SERVING SUGGESTION:
Enjoy with Fever-Tree Mediterranean Tonic Water.

The Cardrona
DISTILLERY
NEW ZEALAND

The Source Gin
47% ABV

A modern dry style gin, The Source Pure Cardrona Gin includes locally foraged rosehip among their botanicals, which was first brought to the Cardrona Valley by Chinese immigrants during the gold rush.

DISTILLERY:
Cardrona Distillery, Cardrona

BOTANICALS:
Juniper, Rosehip, Angelica Root, Coriander Seed, Lemon Zest, Orange Zest & Others

TASTING NOTES:
Complex florals, soft juniper and orange lead the nose, rosehip, citrus and juniper are accented by tropical fruit notes from grain base spirit on the palate, warming orange to finish.

SERVING SUGGESTION:
Enjoy with Fever-Tree Mediterranean Tonic Water.

CHEMISTRY
LONDON DRY GIN

Chemistry London Dry Gin
44% ABV

A modern Dry style gin, Chemistry London Dry Gin was designed at a molecular level to bring out and balance its flavours and is bottled in post-consumer recycled glass, or 'Wild Glass'.

DISTILLERY:
Chemistry Gin, Wellington

BOTANICALS:
Juniper, Coriander Seed, Angelica Root, Lemon, Sichuan Peppercorn, Sage & Seaweed

TASTING NOTES:
Prominent juniper with underlying green herbs and pepper on the nose, coriander and angelica lead with strong juniper on the palate, building hot Sichuan pepper with lemon to finish.

SERVING SUGGESTION:
Enjoy with Fever-Tree Premium Indian Tonic Water.

Curiosity Gin - Classic
40% ABV

A modern dry style gin, Curiosity Gin Classic is their take on the classic London gin, it was made to be enjoyed on any occasion, be it in a martini, G&T, Negroni, Tom Collins, or more.

DISTILLERY:
The Spirits Workshop Distillery, Christchurch

BOTANICALS:
Juniper, Coriander Seed, Angelica Root, Orris Root, Cinnamon, Liquorice, Manuka Leaf, Citrus, Pink Peppercorn & Rose Petal

TASTING NOTES:
Herbaceous florals, fruity notes and coriander on the nose, soft juniper and candied citrus with peppercorn and orris on the palate, developing spice and citrus to finish.

SERVING SUGGESTION:
Enjoy with Fever-Tree Elderflower Tonic Water.

Curiosity Gin - Curious Dry
40% ABV

A modern Dry style Gin, Curiosity Gin Curious Dry is designed for the traditional gin drinker, made with the finest imported juniper and just four other botanicals, all of which are native to New Zealand.

DISTILLERY:
The Spirits Workshop Distillery, Christchurch

BOTANICALS:
Juniper, Tarata, Kawakawa, Horopito & Manuka

TASTING NOTES:
Light juniper and kawakawa with horopito on the nose, soft juniper with green peppery heat and savoury spice on the palate, light earthy sweetness to finish.

SERVING SUGGESTION:
Enjoy with Fever-Tree Mediterranean Tonic Water.

DANCING SANDS DISTILLERY

Dancing Sands Dry Gin
44% ABV

A modern dry style gin, Dancing Sands Dry Gin is double distilled and vapour infused with eight botanicals, including green Manuka leaves, before being blended with water from the pristine Te Waikoropupu Springs.

DISTILLERY:
Dancing Sands Distillery, Takaka

BOTANICALS:
Juniper, Coriander Seed, Angelica Root, Manuka, Cardamom, Peppercorn, Almond & Liquorice Root

TASTING NOTES:
Dry pine with a herbal fragrance on the nose, sweet nutty character with pine resin, earthy liquorice and pepper on the palate, drying cedar and warming pepper to finish.

SERVING SUGGESTION:
Enjoy with Fever-Tree Aromatic Tonic Water.

Denzien Our Coast
42% ABV

A modern dry style gin, Denzien Our Coast Gin calls upon New Zealand's coastal and island identities by using native kelp and Marlborough sea salt as botanicals.

DISTILLERY:
Denzien Urban Distillery, Wellington

BOTANICALS:
Juniper, Sea Salt, Kelp, Black Cardamom, White Peppercorn, Wormwood, Coriander Seed, Angelica Root, Fennel Seed, Liquorice & Orris Root

TASTING NOTES:
Gentle white pepper and juniper on the nose, juniper and soft pepper continue with a salinity character on the palate, developing sweet fennel and pepper to finish.

SERVING SUGGESTION:
Enjoy with Fever-Tree Mediterranean Tonic Water.

Denzien Te Aro Dry

42% ABV

A modern dry style gin, Denzien Te Aro Dry Gin is based on a London Dry Gin with a Kiwi twist and was their first release, made to be a versatile and approachable city gin.

DISTILLERY:
Denzien Urban Distillery, Wellington

BOTANICALS:
Juniper, Horopito, Kawakawa, Lemon Peel, Orange Peel, Coriander Seed, Fennel Seed, Angelica Root, Liquorice & Orris Root

TASTING NOTES:
Orange peel, fresh fennel and subtle juniper drive the nose, roasted fennel, soft juniper and bush pepper on the palate, earthy bush leaves lead a dry unctuous finish.

SERVING SUGGESTION:
Enjoy with Fever-Tree Premium Indian Tonic Water.

duo Citrine Gin

41% ABV

A modern dry style gin, duo Citrine Artisan Distilled Gin is nano-distilled and designed to celebrate the complexity of New Zealand citrus, named for the Citrine gemstone which is a symbol of friendship and happiness.

DISTILLERY:
duo Distilleries, Rotorua

BOTANICALS:
Juniper, Coriander Seed, Liquorice, Angelica Root, Cassia, Orris Root, Fennel Seed, Cardamom, Pink Peppercorn, Lime, Lemon & Orange

TASTING NOTES:
Bold zingy citrus with coriander on the nose, dominant sweet orange and lemon with fennel on the palate, sweet oily orange lingers to finish.

SERVING SUGGESTION:
Enjoy with Fever-Tree Refreshingly Light Indian Tonic Water.

duo Heliodor London Dry Reserve Gin

42% ABV

A modern dry style gin, duo Heliodor London Dry Reserve Gin is nano-distilled, showcasing locally grown Buddha's Hand citrus and named for the Heliodor gemstone that translates as 'a gift from the sun'.

DISTILLERY:
Duo Distilleries, Rotorua

BOTANICALS:
Juniper, Coriander Seed, Liquorice, Angelica Root, Cassia, Orris Root, Fennel Seed, Cardamom, Pink Peppercorn, Lime, Lemon, Orange & Buddha's Hand

TASTING NOTES:
Tart lime, powdered cinnamon and peppercorn on the nose, light juniper and sweet green fennel with lime on the palate, hot cardamom spice with coriander to finish.

SERVING SUGGESTION:
Enjoy with Fever-Tree Mediterranean Tonic Water.

duo Moonstone London Dry Gin

40% ABV

A modern Dry style Gin, duo Moonstone London Dry Gin is nano-distilled, was their first gin, and named for the Moonstone, which is associated with new beginnings.

DISTILLERY:
Duo Distilleries, Rotorua

BOTANICALS:
Juniper, Coriander Seed, Liquorice, Angelica Root, Cassia, Orris Root, Fennel Seed, Cardamom, Pink Peppercorn, Lime, Lemon & Orange

TASTING NOTES:
Pronounced peppercorn with juniper and coriander on the nose, initial spikes of citrus with green fennel and orange on the palate, pink peppercorn takes over with orange to finish.

SERVING SUGGESTION:
Enjoy with Fever-Tree Premium Indian Tonic Water.

ELSEWHERE

TRIPLE GIN — HAND CRAFTED

Elsewhere North Canterbury Triple Gin

42% ABV

A modern dry style gin, Elsewhere North Canterbury Triple Gin is a limited edition that takes inspiration from the region it is named after, paying tribute to the expressive Rieslings that are made their.

DISTILLERY:
Elsewhere Gin, Christchurch

BOTANICALS:
Juniper, Coriander Seed, Angelica Root, Orange Blossom, Lime Leaf, Kawakawa, Liquorice, Tangelo Peel, Bay Leaf, Lavender, Rose, Olive, Wakame Seaweed & Glasnevin Gravel

TASTING NOTES:
Earthy roots and vibrant lime with kawakawa undertones on the nose, light juniper, soft kawakawa and developing earthy roots on the palate, pepper spice and floral citrus to finish.

SERVING SUGGESTION:
Enjoy with Fever-Tree Refreshingly Light Indian Tonic Water.

EXHIBIT A
(Est. 2020)

Exhibit A Gin (No.580)
42% ABV

A modern dry style gin, Exhibit A No.580 is made using collected rainwater and a vegan base spirit all presented in a bottle handmade by sculptor Gidon Bing.

DISTILLERY:
imagaination, Reikorangi

BOTANICALS:
Juniper, Citrus, Green Tea, Cardamom & Others

TASTING NOTES:
Menthol tones with green spice on the nose, pronounced heat with pithy lemon peel and cardamom on the palate, hints of green tea to finish.

SERVING SUGGESTION:
Enjoy with Fever-Tree Refreshingly Light Indian Tonic Water.

Forth Luck Premium Gin

40% ABV

A modern dry style Gin, Forth Luck Premium Gin is crafted in small batches of 100 bottles at a time for veteran gin drinkers, made with a sugar cane base spirit that is distilled six times.

DISTILLERY:
Forth Luck Distillery, Christchurch

BOTANICALS:
Juniper, Coriander Seed, Orris Root, Angelica Root, Liquorice, Cassia, Cubeb, Lemon, Orange & Lavender

TASTING NOTES:
Strong base spirit notes with hints of cassia on the nose, initial juniper with sharp lemon and heated spice on the palate, liquorice drives the finish with hints of suagr cane.

SERVING SUGGESTION:
Enjoy with Fever-Tree Premium Indian Tonic Water.

Forth Luck NZ Dry Gin

40% ABV

A modern dry style gin, Forth Luck NZ Dry Gin is their version of a traditional London Dry gin, keeping true to its rich history, and is made to be a starting point for those new to gin.

DISTILLERY:
Forth Luck Distillery, Christchurch

BOTANICALS:
Juniper, Coriander Seed, Orange, Lemon, Cubeb, Liquorice, Angelica Root & Cassia

---

TASTING NOTES:
Earthy cassia and hints of woody spice on the nose, earthy root tones and supporting angelica leading to strong orange on the palate, cassia spice leads a quick finish.

SERVING SUGGESTION:
Enjoy with Fever-Tree Premium Indian Tonic Water.

Good George Aotearoa Dry Gin

40% ABV

A modern Dry style Gin, Good George Aotearoa Dry Gin is designed to evoke the idea of a laid-back Aotearoan lifestyle and be enjoyed while taking a pause from busy work or crazy life.

DISTILLERY:
Good George Distillery, Hamilton

BOTANICALS:
Juniper, Coriander Seed, Angelica Root, Rosehip, Liquorice, Pink Peppercorn, Mandarin, Star Anise & Cardamom

TASTING NOTES:
Unmistakable mandarin with pronounced pepper on the nose, cardamom, star anise and liquorice dominate the palate, mellowing pink peppercorn heat to finish.

SERVING SUGGESTION:
Enjoy with Fever-Tree Aromatic Tonic Water.

Good George Lemon Gin

40% ABV

A Modern Dry style Gin, Good George Lemon Gin is a citrus twist on their Aotearoa Dry Gin, designed with the idea of only needing to add ice and tonic rather than having to also get out a cutting board and lemon.

DISTILLERY:
Good George Distillery, Hamilton

BOTANICALS:
Juniper, Coriander Seed, Angelica Root, Rosehip, Liquorice, Star Anise, Liquorice, Orange Peel & Lemon Peel

TASTING NOTES:
Fresh lemon peel leads the nose, layered citrus morphs into distinct lemon peel with warming juniper on the palate, long warming citrus and pine to finish.

SERVING SUGGESTION:
Enjoy with Fever-Tree Refreshingly Light Indian Tonic Water.

Good George For F***'s Sake 2021 Gin

45% ABV

A modern dry style gin, Good George For ****'s Sake 2021 Gin embodies their feelings about world events in 2021 while viewing their cups as half-full and having something to top them up.

DISTILLERY:
Good George Distillery, Hamilton

BOTANICALS:
Juniper, Coriander Seed, Angelica Root, Rosehip, Liquorice, Pink Peppercorn, Mandarin, Star Anise & Cardamom

TASTING NOTES:
Oily mandarin, cardamom and star anise lead the nose, bold cardamom heat with light citrus on the palate, cardamom continues with mellowing anise to finish.

SERVING SUGGESTION:
Enjoy with Fever-Tree Premium Indian Tonic Water.

Good George What's F***ing Next 2022 Gin

40% ABV

A modern dry style gin, Good George What's F***ing Next 2022 Gin continues their series of tongue in cheek releases regarding world affairs with the sentiment that whatever happens, you always raise a glass or two.

DISTILLERY:
Good George Distillery, Hamilton

BOTANICALS:
Juniper, Coriander Seed, Angelica Root, Rosehip, Liquorice, Pink Peppercorn, Mandarin, Star Anise & Cardamom

TASTING NOTES:
Mandarin peel, light juniper and classic spice on the nose, cardamom and integrated mandarin with peppery heat on the palate, strong mandarin with warming spice to finish.

SERVING SUGGESTION:
Enjoy with Fever-Tree Premium Indian Tonic Water.

HERRICK CREEK

Moose Lake Classic New Zealand Gin

46% ABV

A modern dry style gin, Herrick Creek Moose Lake Classic New Zealand Gin uses a corn mash moonshine made from scratch as its base, then rectified in a pot still, and named for the small lake at the centre of the fabled moose sightings in Fiordland.

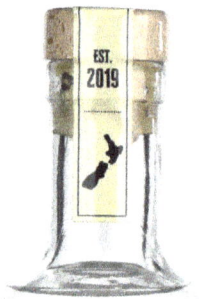

DISTILLERY:
Herrick Creek Distillery, Christchurch

BOTANICALS:
Juniper, Coriander Seed, Angelica Root, Lemon Peel, Cinnamon & Almond

TASTING NOTES:
Grain like notes with light spice on the nose, base notes continue with coriander, angelica and strong spice on the palate, hints of earthiness and grain lingering to finish.

SERVING SUGGESTION:
Enjoy with Fever-Tree Premium Indian Tonic Water.

Pink Grapefruit & Kawakawa Gin

44% ABV

A modern dry style gin, Holland Road Pink Grapefruit & Kawakawa London Dry Gin features a blend of traditional botanicals alongside seasonal pink grapefruit, kawakawa, and a touch of Kanuka honey.

DISTILLERY:
Holland Road Distillery, Eureka

BOTANICALS:
Juniper, Coriander Seed, Angelica Root, Liquorice, Cassia, Orris Root, Kawakawa, Grapefruit & Kanuka Honey

TASTING NOTES:
Kawakawa, tart grapefruit backed and juniper on the nose, juniper leads with orris, liquorice and citrus peel on the palate, peppery heat with gentle spice to finish.

SERVING SUGGESTION:
Enjoy with Fever-Tree Mediterranean Tonic Water.

Sauvignon Blanc & Green Tea Gin

42% ABV

A modern dry style gin, Holland Road Sauvignon Blanc & Green Tea London Dry Gin features a blend of traditional botanicals alongside freshly picked organic green tea and a vibrant Sauvignon Blanc.

DISTILLERY:
Holland Road Distillery, Eureka

BOTANICALS:
Juniper, Coriander Seed, Angelica Root, Liquorice, Cassia, Sauvignon Blanc, Green Tea, Orris Root, Nutmeg, Clove, Cardamom, Lemon, Bitter Orange & Ginger

TASTING NOTES:
Classic baking spice, pithy orange and ginger on the nose, cassia and cardamom with tea leaves on the palate, rolling to warming clove, liquorice and orange to finish.

SERVING SUGGESTION:
Enjoy with Fever-Tree Mediterranean Tonic Water.

Wild Ginseng & Manuka Honey Gin

47% ABV

A modern dry style gin, Holland Road Wild Ginseng & Manuka Honey London Dry Gin features a blend of traditional botanicals alongside freshly harvested wild ginseng, raw Manuka honey, and a hint of green yuzu.

DISTILLERY:
Holland Road Distillery, Eureka

BOTANICALS:
Juniper, Coriander Seed, Angelica Root, Liquorice, Cassia, Ginseng, Raw Manuka Honey, Lemon, Bitter Orange & Yuzu

TASTING NOTES:
Intriguing ginseng with juniper and coriander on the nose, upfront juniper with cassia and orange on the palate, lingering angelica and cassia to finish.

SERVING SUGGESTION:
Enjoy with Fever-Tree Mediterranean Tonic Water.

Humdinger Citrus Gin
40% ABV

A modern dry style gin, Humdinger Citrus Gin is made using many of the same botanicals as their Dry Gin with a greater focus on the fresh lemon and orange peel they source from Gisborne.

DISTILLERY:
Humdinger Distillery, Geraldine

BOTANICALS:
Juniper, Barley, Coriander Seed, Nutmeg, Angelica Root, Ginger, Lemon Peel & Orange Peel

TASTING NOTES:
Fresh citrus with faint spice on the nose, subtle hints of ginger, baking spice and sweet orange on the palate, angelica and ginger to finish.

SERVING SUGGESTION:
Enjoy with Fever-Tree Mediterranean Tonic Water.

Humdinger Dry Gin

40% ABV

A modern dry style gin, Humdinger Dry Gin is distilled using the London Dry method in a balance between British methodology and Humdinger's flair for ingenuity.

DISTILLERY:
Humdinger Distillery, Geraldine

BOTANICALS:
Juniper, Barley, Coriander Seed, Nutmeg, Liquorice, Angelica Root, Ginger, Lemon Peel & Orange Peel

TASTING NOTES:
Coriander, dry root spice and light citrus on the nose, initial spikes of juniper backed by coriander and ginger on the palate, oily citrus with warming ginger to finish.

SERVING SUGGESTION:
Enjoy with Fever-Tree Aromatic Tonic Water.

Reikorangi Triple Distilled New Zealand Dry Gin

42% ABV

A modern Dry style gin, imagination Reikorangi Triple Distilled Dry Gin aims to create a rustic craft edge with the use of whole oranges, lemons, and limes among its other botanicals.

DISTILLERY:
imagination, Reikorangi

BOTANICALS:
Juniper, Coriander Seed, Cinnamon, Liquorice, Orris Root, Orange, Lime, Lemon & Manuka

TASTING NOTES:
Peppery spice with coriander and pronounced cinnamon on the nose, liquorice leads with earthy base notes and zesty citrus on the palate, heavy spice lingers to finish.

SERVING SUGGESTION:
Enjoy with Fever-Tree Aromatic Tonic Water.

Juno Emily
44% ABV

A modern dry style gin, Juno Emily is a full-bodied botanical gin named for the artist and poet Emily Cumming Harris, that takes inspiration from her love of all things botanical.

DISTILLERY:
Begin Distilling, New Plymouth

BOTANICALS:
Juniper, Coriander Seed, Angelica Root, Orris Root, Cassia, Orange, Cardamom, Nutmeg, Manuka Honey, Lime Blossom & Chamomile

TASTING NOTES:
Lime blossom, light hay and juniper on the nose, earthy musk with bold citrus, drying tea and consistent juniper on the palate, complex florals with citrus to finish.

SERVING SUGGESTION:
Enjoy with Fever-Tree Refreshingly Light Indian Tonic Water.

Juno Extra Fine

40% ABV

A modern dry style gin, Juno Extra Fine Gin is their signature gin, made with a range of fresh locally-grown botanicals to be the perfect base for building cocktails as well as a classic G&T or martini.

DISTILLERY:
Begin Distilling, New Plymouth

BOTANICALS:
Juniper, Coriander Seed, Angelica Root, Orris Root, Makrut Lime Leaf, Manuka, Orange, Black Peppercorn, Cardamom & Cassia

TASTING NOTES:
Fresh lime leaf, earthy roots and light pine on the nose, juniper leads with lime leaf, cassia and angelica on the palate, peppery spice and lime leaf linger to finish.

SERVING SUGGESTION:
Enjoy with Fever-Tree Mediterranean Tonic Water.

Juno Jean
44% ABV

A classic dry gin, Juno Jean is a gin named for the medical pioneer and women's advocate Jean Sandel that takes on the flavours of summer.

DISTILLERY:
Begin Distilling, New Plymouth

BOTANICALS:
Juniper, Coriander Seed, Angelica Root, Orris Root, Cassia, Orange, Cardamom, Nutmeg & Horopito

TASTING NOTES:
Lightly toasted coriander, dark roots and orange on the nose, juniper forward with supporting citrus, coriander and orris on the palate, warming pepper with bitter citrus to finish.

SERVING SUGGESTION:
Enjoy with Fever-Tree Premium Indian Tonic Water.

GIN

Juno Monica
44% ABV

A modern dry style gin, Juno Monica is a 44% ABV expression of a full-flavoured citrus gin developed in collaboration with New Plymouth's Govett-Brewster Art Gallery and Len Lye Centre to celebrate Monica Brewster, an advocate for women's rights, the environment, pacifism, and the arts.

DISTILLERY:
Begin Distilling, New Plymouth

BOTANICALS:
Juniper, Coriander Seed, Angelica Root, Orris Root, Cassia, Orange, Cardamom, Nutmeg, Lemongrass, Lemon Verbena & Makrut Lime Leaf

TASTING NOTES:
Bold lime leaf and light coriander on the nose, strong lime leaf continues with warming orange and coriander on the palate, waxy lime leaf with mellowing spice to finish.

SERVING SUGGESTION:
Enjoy with Fever-Tree Mediterranean Tonic Water.

Monica Gin

40% ABV

A modern dry style gin, Monica Gin is a 40% ABV expression of a full-flavoured citrus gin developed in collaboration with New Plymouth's Govett-Brewster Art Gallery and Len Lye Centre to celebrate Monica Brewster, an advocate for women's rights, the environment, pacifism, and the arts.

DISTILLERY:
Begin Distilling, New Plymouth

BOTANICALS:
Juniper, Coriander Seed, Angelica Root, Orris Root, Cassia, Orange, Cardamom, Nutmeg, Lemongrass, Lemon Verbena & Makrut Lime Leaf

TASTING NOTES:
Bold makrut, coriander, and angelica on the nose, makrut and coriander continue with complex dark roots and cardamom on the palate, mellowing spice with warming lime leaf settle to finish.

SERVING SUGGESTION:
Enjoy with Fever-Tree Mediterranean Tonic Water.

GIN

Juno Summer 2022

44% ABV

A modern dry style gin, Juno Summer 2022 Seasonal Gin is designed to be a refreshing gin for long hot summer days, featuring artwork by Victoria Pickles on its bottle.

DISTILLERY:
Begin Distilling, New Plymouth

BOTANICALS:
Juniper, Coriander Seed, Angelica Root, Orris Root, Cassia, Orange, Cardamom, Nutmeg, Seville Orange & Gentian Root

TASTING NOTES:
Aromatic juniper, sharp orange and earthy roots on the nose, sharp citrus with pronounced angelica and juniper on the palate, warming pepper and bitter orange to finish.

SERVING SUGGESTION:
Enjoy with Fever-Tree Premium Indian Tonic Water.

1963 Citrus Gin

40% ABV

A modern Dry style gin, 1963 Citrus Gin is a blend of their Premium Dry Gin with additional citrus, made to be ideal for citrus lovers and great in cocktails.

DISTILLERY:
Kim Clifford Distillery, Cromwell

BOTANICALS:
Juniper, Coriander Seed, Whole Lemon, Whole Lime & Whole Orange

TASTING NOTES:
Bright lemon backed by pleasant coriander on the nose, strong orange with light coriander and lemon on the palate, subtle sweetness mellows to finish.

SERVING SUGGESTION:
Enjoy with Fever-Tree Refreshingly Light Indian Tonic Water.

KIWI SPIRIT DISTILLERY

Championz Gin

40% ABV

A modern dry style gin, Championz Gin is a dry gin made with water from the nearby Te Waikoropupu Springs, often considered the clearest spring water in the world.

DISTILLERY:
Kiwi Spirit Distillery, Motupipi

BOTANICALS:
Juniper, Angelica Root, Liquorice & Others

TASTING NOTES:
Minty freshness, lemon and hints of eucalyptus on the nose, light mint continues with a touch of spice and citrus on the palate, lasting dry yet heated finish.

SERVING SUGGESTION:
Enjoy with Fever-Tree Refreshingly Light Indian Tonic Water.

KIWI SPIRIT DISTILLERY

Delightful Dry Gin

40% ABV

A modern dry style gin, Kiwi Spirit Distillery Delightful Dry Gin is made using a variety of botanicals, including lavender and lemon, which are grown on the distillery's grounds and picked fresh.

DISTILLERY:
Kiwi Spirit Distillery, Motupipi

BOTANICALS:
Juniper, Lavender, Lemon & Others

TASTING NOTES:
Savoury and herbaceous characters lead the nose, slightly sweet earthy spice with a light touch of citrus on the palate, mellowing baking spice to finish.

SERVING SUGGESTION:
Enjoy with Fever-Tree Mediterranean Tonic Water.

Gin & Bare It Original Gin

40% ABV

A modern dry style gin, Gin & Bare It Original Gin is Lammermoor Distillery's flagship gin, a marriage of passion and pleasure featuring classic botanicals alongside others like Central Otago thyme.

DISTILLERY:
Lammermoor Distillery, Lammermoor

BOTANICALS:
Juniper & Others

TASTING NOTES:
Clean light coriander and juniper on the nose, subtle coriander and light cassia on the palate, sweetness mellows to finish.

SERVING SUGGESTION:
Enjoy with Fever-Tree Mediterranean Tonic Water.

Laughing Club Gin
44% ABV

A modern dry style gin, Laughing Club Gin takes inspiration from the roaring 20s, luxury Raffles Hotel in Singapore, and a legend about a raucous club by the same name.

DISTILLERY:
Kiwi Spirit Distillery, Motupipi

BOTANICALS:
Juniper, Coriander Seed, Peppercorn, Cubeb, Lemon, Orris Root & Liquorice

TASTING NOTES:
Dry citrus with light juniper on the nose, juniper and coriander develop with some hot pepper and earthy roots on the palate, quick citrus to finish.

SERVING SUGGESTION:
Enjoy with Fever-Tree Refreshingly Light Indian Tonic Water.

Lighthouse Gin Original

42% ABV

A classic dry style gin, Lighthouse Gin's recipe was perfected over many years with a unique blend of nine botanicals and was the first ever New Zealand gin to be selected for presentation by the UK's Craft Gin Club.

DISTILLERY:
Lighthouse Distillery, Martinborough

BOTANICALS:
Juniper, Coriander Seed, Yen Ben Lemon Zest, Navel Orange Zest, Cinnamon, Almond, Cassia, Orris Root & Liquorice

TASTING NOTES:
Lemon peel, juniper and baking spice lead the nose, dry juniper, orange sweetness and classic spice on the palate, mellowing creamy nut character with lasting citrus to finish.

SERVING SUGGESTION:
Enjoy with Fever-Tree Aromatic Tonic Water.

LTD Issue No. 01 Botanical Gin
45% ABV

A modern dry style gin, LTD Issue No.01 Botanical Gin is a botanically-rich dry gin that features an artwork by Chimp on the bottle called 'Moment' with two faces mirroring each other through the glass, as though connecting through the gin itself.

DISTILLERY:
Elemental Distillers, Blenheim

BOTANICALS:
Juniper, Coriander Seed, Grapefruit Zest, Orris Root, Angelica Root, Chamomile Flower, Manuka Leaf & Giant Kelp

TASTING NOTES:
Juniper, grapefruit peel and chamomile undertones on the nose, initial coriander and angelica with a juniper backbone on the palate, drying chamomile and light juniper to finish.

SERVING SUGGESTION:
Enjoy with Fever-Tree Refreshingly Light Indian Tonic Water.

The Racketeer London Dry Gin
42% ABV

A classic dry style gin, The Racketeer London Dry Gin is a combination of their favourite botanicals, including almond and rosehip among other more traditional ones.

DISTILLERY:
LongShot Distillery, Rolleston

BOTANICALS:
Juniper, Coriander Seed, Almond, Lemon, Orange, Elderberry & Rosehip

TASTING NOTES:
Bright lemon, soft florals and light coriander on the nose, sweet lemon leads with strong coriander and soft spice on the palate, continuing lemon with coriander to finish.

SERVING SUGGESTION:
Enjoy with Fever-Tree Premium Indian Tonic Water.

NDC Art Deco Gin
40% ABV

A classic dry style gin, NDC Art Deco Gin is designed to be an elegant but fine summer gin, featuring Hawke's Bay citrus and donating 15% of its profits to the Art Deco Trust in Napier.

DISTILLERY:
The National Distillery Co., Napier

BOTANICALS:
Juniper, Coriander Seed, Angelica Root, Cardamom, Orris Root, Cassia, Liquorice, Orange Peel, Lemon Peel & Lime Peel

TASTING NOTES:
Bold cassia and coriander with light citrus on the nose, leading citrus and juniper with liquorice and cassia on the palate, lingering earthy spice to finish.

SERVING SUGGESTION:
Enjoy with Fever-Tree Premium Indian Tonic Water.

NDC New Zealand Dry Gin

42% ABV

A classic dry style gin, NDC's New Zealand Dry Gin is made using classic botanicals like coriander seed and cassia bark alongside others including lemon peel.

DISTILLERY:
The National Distillery Co., Napier

BOTANICALS:
Juniper, Coriander Seed, Angelica Root, Cardamom, Orris Root, Cassia, Lemon Peel & Liquorice

TASTING NOTES:
Earthy root botanicals on the nose, resinous juniper with bitter lemon peel on the palate, peppery heat leads a long finish.

SERVING SUGGESTION:
Enjoy with Fever-Tree Refreshingly Light Indian Tonic Water.

No8 Distillery Dunners Dry
42% ABV

A modern dry style gin, the No8 Distillery Dunners Dry takes cues from its two makers' culinary histories with botanicals from the Mediterranean and Aotearoa included in its blend.

DISTILLERY:
No8 Distillery, Dunedin

BOTANICALS:
Juniper, Coriander Seed, Angelica Root, Orris Root, Lemon, Lime, Mandarin, Kawakawa, Tarata, Thyme, Sage & Basil

TASTING NOTES:
Pronounced kawakawa and tarata with subtle juniper on the nose, bold sage with a peppery burst and leafy forest floor elements on the palate, savoury herbs linger to finish.

SERVING SUGGESTION:
Enjoy with Fever-Tree Mediterranean Tonic Water.

Papaiti Gin Whanganui Dry

45% ABV

A modern dry style gin, Papaiti Gin Whanganui Dry is single-shot distilled in the tradition of a London Dry gin, featuring a combination of traditional and contemporary botanicals to create a modern twist.

DISTILLERY:
Papaiti Gin, Upokongaro

BOTANICALS:
Juniper, Coriander Seed, Angelica Root, Pink Peppercorn, Mint, Almond, Lemon Peel & Orange Peel

TASTING NOTES:
Lemon and coriander with lifted mint on the nose, lemon, juniper and mint lead with supporting earthy spice on the palate, warming mint and lemon to finish.

SERVING SUGGESTION:
Enjoy with Fever-Tree Mediterranean Tonic Water.

Papaka Road Gin
42% ABV

A modern dry style gin, Papaka Road Gin aims to evoke the warmth, refreshment, and seclusion of the Tutukaka Coast with fresh, seasonal citrus zest and natural botanicals.

DISTILLERY:
Papaka Road Distillery, Ngunguru

BOTANICALS:
Juniper, Coriander Seed, Angelica Root, Liquorice, Seasonal Citrus & Others

TASTING NOTES:
Pronounced liquorice, sweet baking spice and marmalade on the nose, baking spice continues with citrus peel on the palate, lingering liquorice sweetness on the finish.

SERVING SUGGESTION:
Enjoy with Fever-Tree Aromatic Tonic Water.

Pink & White Geothermal Gin White

45% ABV

A modern dry style Gin, Pink & White Geothermal Gin White is modelled after a classic Victorian using a relatively simple recipe and the goal of creating a "Gin that tastes like Gin".

DISTILLERY:
Pink & White - Geothermal Gin, Rotorua

BOTANICALS:
Juniper, Coriander Seed, Angelica Root, Lemon & Others

TASTING NOTES:
Soft spice and earthy coriander on the nose, subtle juniper, mentholic mint and forest floor elements on the palate, lingering minty heat accents earthiness to finish.

SERVING SUGGESTION:
Enjoy with Fever-Tree Premium Indian Tonic Water

Pollen Gin
43% ABV

A modern dry style gin, Pollen Gin was designed with allergy sufferers in mind, containing no sulphites and a low histamine content, made using natural artesian water and a blend of organic botanicals which are both macerated and infused.

DISTILLERY:
Elemental Distillers, Blenheim

BOTANICALS:
Juniper, Coriander Seed, Orange Flesh, Angelica Root, Orris Root, Rosemary, Cassia, Makrut Lime & Cardamom

---

TASTING NOTES:
Lime leaf, juniper and balanced spice on the nose, juniper leads with citrus and perfumed orris on the palate, cassia and cardamom develop with orange throughout to finish.

SERVING SUGGESTION:
Enjoy with Fever-Tree Premium Indian Tonic Water.

GUIDE TO NEW ZEALAND GIN — VOL. 3 — TASTERS' PICK

CRAFT DISTILLERS OF MARTINBOROUGH

Reid + Reid Native Gin
42% ABV

A modern dry style gin, Reid + Reid Native Gin is the result of a two year mission foraging the landscapes of New Zealand for the aromatic native plants that best compliment a classic dry gin, including Kawakawa, Manuka, and Horopito.

DISTILLERY:
Reid + Reid Distillery, Martinborough

BOTANICALS:
Juniper, Coriander Seed, Angelica Root, Liquorice, Orris Root, Fennel Seed, Nutmeg, Cassia, Cardamom, Orange Peel, Kawakawa, Horopito & Manuka

TASTING NOTES:
Kawakawa and earthy spice lead the nose, fragrant kawakawa, Manuka and horopito pepper on the palate, developing native herbs linger for a heated finish.

SERVING SUGGESTION:
Enjoy with Fever-Tree Mediterranean Tonic Water.

CRAFT DISTILLERS OF MARTINBOROUGH

Reid + Reid Rev. Dawson's Gin
42% ABV

A modern dry style gin, Reid + Reid Rev. Dawson's Gin is distilled using the 'one shot' method and is named tongue-in-cheek after one of New Zealand's leading prohibitionists from the early 1900's who also happens to be the founders' great, great grandfather.

DISTILLERY:
Reid + Reid Distillery, Martinborough

BOTANICALS:
Juniper, Coriander Seed, Angelica Root, Orris Root, Fennel Seed, Cassia, Orange & Grapefruit

TASTING NOTES:
Striking grapefruit with coriander on the nose, sweet marmalade citrus with developing root spice on the palate, earthy roots continue with added heat to finish.

SERVING SUGGESTION:
Enjoy with Fever-Tree Mediterranean Tonic Water.

RIFTERS

BOUTIQUE NEW ZEALAND GIN
HANDCRAFTED.

Rifters Original Dry Gin

42% ABV

A classic dry style gin, Rifters Original Dry Gin is made using a selection of locally foraged botanicals amongst others and presented in a bottle made from 20%+ recycled glass.

DISTILLERY:
Arrowtown Distillery, Arrowtown

BOTANICALS:
Juniper, Coriander Seed, Angelica Root, Liquorice, Orris Root, Cardamom, Orange Peel, Lemon Peel & Others

TASTING NOTES:
Classic juniper, coriander and orris on the nose, sweet orange with pine and pronounced earthiness on the palate, lasting citrus, coriander and orris to finish.

SERVING SUGGESTION:
Enjoy with Fever-Tree Premium Indian Tonic Water.

Roots Marlborough Dry Gin

45% ABV

A modern dry style gin, Roots Marlborough Dry Gin is batch distilled after a 24-hour activated maceration using a sustainable neutral base spirit and New Zealand botanicals.

DISTILLERY:
Elemental Distillers, Blenheim

BOTANICALS:
Juniper, Grapefruit Zest, Coriander Seed, Hop, Kawakawa Fruit & Gorse Flower

TASTING NOTES:
Grapefruit, kawakawa, and funky green notes on the nose, bitter hops, grapefruit peel and kawakawa accented by a juniper on the palate, developing kawakawa and bitter notes to finish.

SERVING SUGGESTION:
Enjoy with Fever-Tree Mediterranean Tonic Water.

Lovers Leap Dry Gin
43% ABV

A modern Dry style Gin, Sandymount Distillery Lovers Leap Dry Gin is named after a nearby spot on the Otago Peninsula coastline and created as a nod to the London Dry style with a hint of New Zealand flavour.

DISTILLERY:
Sandymount Distillery,
Otago Peninsula

BOTANICALS:
Juniper, Coriander Seed,
Cardamom, Cinnamon, Orris Root,
Angelica Root, Citrus & Manuka

TASTING NOTES:
Striking coriander seed, orris and citrus peel on the nose, bold citrus and coriander lead with a touch of bitter earth on the palate, light florals linger to finish.

SERVING SUGGESTION:
Enjoy with Fever-Tree
Mediterranean Tonic Water.

SCAPEGRACE
NEW ZEALAND DISTILLING CO

Scapegrace Classic
42.2% ABV

A London dry style gin, Scapegrace Dry Gin epitomises the nature of a classic gin, made using 12 botanicals of which juniper and citrus peel shine through, and was one of the first New Zealand gins to receive global recognition.

DISTILLERY:
Scapegrace Distilling Co., Bendigo

BOTANICALS:
Juniper, Lemon Peel, Orange Peel, Coriander Seed, Cardamom, Nutmeg, Angelica Root, Liquorice, Orris Root, Clove, Cinnamon & Cassia

TASTING NOTES:
Bold citrus leads with subtle baking spice on the nose, intense citrus with warming spice and light juniper on the palate, light spice continues with a clean citrus driven finish.

SERVING SUGGESTION:
Enjoy with Fever-Tree Premium Indian Tonic Water.

SCAPEGRACE
NEW ZEALAND DISTILLING CO

Uncommon Central Otago Early Harvest
42.2% ABV

A modern dry style gin, Scapegrace Uncommon Central Otago Early Harvest uses new season produce from Central Otago after the winter thaw, concentrating floral and stone fruit elements.

— VOL. 3 —
HIGHLY COMMENDED
GUIDE TO NEW ZEALAND GIN

ULTIMATE MIX
DRY MARTINI
GUIDE TO NEW ZEALAND GIN

DISTILLERY:
Scapegrace Distilling Co., Bendigo

BOTANICALS:
Juniper, Lemon Peel, Orange Peel, Coriander Seed, Cardamom, Nutmeg, Angelica Root, Liquorice, Orris Root, Clove, Cinnamon, Cassia, Nectarine, Lavender, Smoked Hay & Pollen

TASTING NOTES:
Gentle smoke, soft coriander and cassia lead the nose, light juniper with smoke elevating baking spice notes on the palate, floral lavender with light smoke lingering to finish.

SERVING SUGGESTION:
Enjoy with Fever-Tree Refreshingly Light Indian Tonic Water.

SCAPEGRACE
NEW ZEALAND DISTILLING CO

Uncommon Hawke's Bay Late Harvest
42.2% ABV

A modern dry style gin, Scapegrace Uncommon Hawke's Bay Late Harvest showcases the seeing out of the summer produce whilst capturing the concentrated and preserved flavours as the crops ready themselves for winter.

DISTILLERY:
Scapegrace Distilling Co., Bendigo

BOTANICALS:
Juniper, Lemon Peel, Orange Peel, Coriander Seed, Cardamom, Nutmeg, Angelica Root, Liquorice, Orris Root, Clove, Cinnamon, Cassia, Raspberry Leaf, Pear & Olive Brine

TASTING NOTES:
Delicate raspberry leaf and baking spice with a touch of hay on the nose, floral honey leads with soft raspberry tea and light earth on the palate, lifted lemon and baking spice to finish.

SERVING SUGGESTION:
Enjoy with Fever-Tree Refreshingly Light Indian Tonic Water.

CHATHAM ISLANDS
BLACK ROBIN™
RARE GIN

Black Robin Rare Gin

43% ABV

A modern dry style gin, Black Robin Rare Gin is five times distilled with a unique blend of botanicals, including some native to New Zealand to honour the Black Robin's heritage. The bottle's Black Robin artwork was originally hand-painted by renowned NZ artist Andrew Barns-Graham.

DISTILLERY:
Distillerie Deinlein, Te Puna

BOTANICALS:
Juniper, Chervil, Watercress, Parsley, Mint, Liquorice, Star Anise, Horopito, Candied Lime Zest, Candied Lemon Zest & Lemongrass

TASTING NOTES:
Candied citrus zest and hints of forest floor on the nose, peppery horopito, light juniper and sweet lemon on the palate, earthy liquorice leads a dry finish.

SERVING SUGGESTION:
Enjoy with Fever-Tree Mediterranean Tonic Water.

Sir Winston Gin Classic
40% ABV

A modern dry style gin, Sir Winston Gin Classic is themed around its namesake, using Churchill's favourite tea, Lapsang, as the feature among its eight botanicals.

DISTILLERY:
1919 Distilling, Auckland

BOTANICALS:
Juniper, Lapsang Tea, Coriander Seed, Cinnamon, Orris Root, Liquorice, Lemon Peel & Orange Peel

TASTING NOTES:
Earthy roots and gentle smoke on the nose, earthy characters continue with supporting coriander, black tea and marmalade-like citrus on the palate, lingering dark roots accented by subtle smoke to finish.

SERVING SUGGESTION:
Enjoy with Fever-Tree Premium Indian Tonic Water.

SOLACE
GIN

Solace London Dry Gin
42.2 % ABV

A classic dry style gin, Solace London Dry Gin pays homage to the London Dry Gin style using a mixture of 13 traditional botanicals.

DISTILLERY:
Kings Liquor, Auckland

BOTANICALS:
Juniper, Coriander Seed, Cassia, Angelica Root, Nutmeg, Citrus Peel, Tangerine, Orris Root, Star Anise, Anise, Lemon, Orange & Cardamom

TASTING NOTES:
Spirit-forward with grassy hints and citrus notes on the nose, sweet and round citrus with light spice on the palate, earthy spice leads a dry finish.

SERVING SUGGESTION:
Enjoy with Fever-Tree Premium Indian Tonic Water.

5 Mile Gin
40% ABV

A modern dry style gin, Taupo Distilling Co. 5 Mile Gin is made in a small 50L still using a combination of maceration and vapour infusion to get the most out of its botanicals, and cut to strength with Tongariro Natural Spring Water.

DISTILLERY:
Taupo Distilling Co., Taupo

BOTANICALS:
Juniper, Coriander Seed, Green Cardamom, Angelica Root, Cassia, Walnut, Dried Lime Peel & Green Peppercorn

TASTING NOTES:
Pronounced cassia and cardamom with earthy tones on the nose, cassia and cardamom continue with angelica on the palate, warming citrus and lasting earthy characters to finish.

SERVING SUGGESTION:
Enjoy with Fever-Tree Premium Indian Tonic Water.

TWELFTH HOUR
— DISTILLERY —

Twelfth Hour Dry Gin
43% ABV

A modern dry style gin, Twelfth Hour Dry Gin is the final result after 22 previous iterations built around the use of makrut lime, which they get home-grown from the garden of their master distiller's mum.

DISTILLERY:
Twelfth Hour Distillery, Auckland

BOTANICALS:
Juniper, Makrut Lime, Coriander Seed, Orange, Lemon & Others

TASTING NOTES:
Unmistakable lime leaf with juniper undertones on the nose, bright lime leaf, green coriander seed and hints of pine on the palate, mentholic hot spice leads a dry finish.

SERVING SUGGESTION:
Enjoy with Fever-Tree Mediterranean Tonic Water.

The Vicar's Son Gin - Classic London Dry
46% ABV

A classic dry style gin, The Vicar's Son Gin is quadruple distilled with 20 vapour infusion extraction cycles using Antipodes Water.

DISTILLERY:
The Vicar's Son, Auckland

BOTANICALS:
Juniper, Lemon Villa Franca Peel, Lime Peel, Nutmeg, Red Pepper, Green Pepper, Almond, Cinnamon, Cardamom, Poppy Seed, Liquorice, Coriander Seed & Angelica Root

TASTING NOTES:
Intense lemon, sweet spice and peppery heat on the nose, cardamom to open with bold lemon, grassy tones and warming spice on the palate, hints of pine with baking spice to finish.

SERVING SUGGESTION:
Enjoy with Fever-Tree Premium Indian Tonic Water.

The Vicar's Son Gin - Ascension
46% ABV

A modern dry style gin,, The Vicar's Son Gin Ascension is quadruple distilled with 20 vapour infusion extraction cycles using Antipodes Water, with a high botanical ratio of 90 grams per litre.

DISTILLERY:
The Vicar's Son, Auckland

BOTANICALS:
Juniper, Grapefruit Peel, Lemon Thyme, Mandarina Bavaria Hop, White Peppercorn, Black Peppercorn, Nutmeg, Almond, Cinnamon, Cardamom, Liquorice, Coriander Seed, Angelica Root & Others

TASTING NOTES:
Juicy bouquet of citrus fruits on the nose, grapefruit peel, pleasant pepper and cardamom on the palate, lifted heat with fruity characters and developing earthiness to finish.

SERVING SUGGESTION:
Enjoy with Fever-Tree Premium Indian Tonic Water.

The Vicar's Son Gin - Revelation
46% ABV

A modern dry style gin,, The Vicar's Son Gin Revelation is made using their own base spirit at a higher percentage than their other gins, at 96%, to achieve a greater neutrality and remove its agricultural note.

DISTILLERY:
The Vicar's Son, Auckland

BOTANICALS:
Juniper, Lemon Villa Franca Peel, Lime Peel, Nutmeg, Red Pepper, Green Pepper, Almond, Cinnamon, Cardamom, Poppy Seed, Liquorice, Coriander Seed, Angelica Root & Ginger

TASTING NOTES:
Candied lemon-lime, cardamom and subtle pepper on the nose, nutmeg and cardamom with savoury pepper and candied citrus on the palate, juicy lemon with ginger and coriander to finish.

SERVING SUGGESTION:
Enjoy with Fever-Tree Premium Indian Tonic Water.

The Vicar's Son Gin - The Holy Spirit
46% ABV

A modern dry style gin,, The Vicar's Son Gin The Holy Spirit is quadruple distilled with 20 vapour infusion cycles using Antipodes water like their original gin, but with botanical differences such as saffron and pink peppercorn.

DISTILLERY:
The Vicar's Son, Auckland

BOTANICALS:
Juniper, Saffron, Pink Peppercorn, Rosemary Flower, Angelica Root, Cassia, Liquorice, Poppy Seed, Cardamom, Nutmeg, Dried Lemonade Lemon Zest & Others

TASTING NOTES:
Sweet citrus with light florals and grain character on the nose, delicate spice and light juniper accented by sweet citrus and tingling pepper on the palate, lingering coriander and light spice heat to finish.

SERVING SUGGESTION:
Enjoy with Fever-Tree Premium Indian Tonic Water.

The Vicar's Son Gin - Without Sin
46% ABV

A modern dry style gin,, The Vicar's Son Gin Without Sin is made using their own base spirit at a higher percentage than their other gins, at 96%, to achieve a greater neutrality and remove its agricultural note which allows its citrus and spice to come through more clearly.

DISTILLERY:
The Vicar's Son, Auckland

BOTANICALS:
Juniper, Lemon Peel, Lime Peel, Nutmeg, Red Pepper, Green Pepper, Almond, Cinnamon, Cardamom, Poppy Seed, Liquorice, Coriander Seed & Angelica Root

TASTING NOTES:
Classic citrus and spice on the nose, juniper with lemon-lime, cinnamon and strong pepper on the palate, pepper carries with a sharp lime lead finish.

SERVING SUGGESTION:
Enjoy with Fever-Tree Premium Indian Tonic Water.

Victor Gin Heavy Botanical
42% ABV

A modern dry style gin, Victor Gin Heavy Botanical looks to early rock n' roll and the idea of using only a few instruments that sound great together by using only the flavours that they love rather than a broad range of botanicals.

DISTILLERY:
Thomson Whisky Distillery, Riverhead

BOTANICALS:
Juniper, Lemon, Lemongrass, Cardamom & Coriander Seed

TASTING NOTES:
Zesty citrus and lemongrass with coriander on the nose, vibrant lemongrass and coriander with citrus on the palate, citrus develops and lingers to finish.

SERVING SUGGESTION:
Enjoy with Fever-Tree Mediterranean Tonic Water.

WAIHEKE DISTILLING CO.

Waiheke Distilling Co. London Dry

42% ABV

A modern Dry style gin, Waiheke Distilling Co. London Dry is designed after the time-honoured classic with notable additions of macadamia and pink peppercorn.

DISTILLERY:
Waiheke Distilling Co., Waiheke

BOTANICALS:
Juniper, Macadamia, Pink Peppercorn, Lemon & Others

TASTING NOTES:
Fragrant nuttiness with lemon and juniper on the nose, slightly sweet with hot pepper and bursting citrus on the palate, earthy roots and peppery heat lead the finish.

SERVING SUGGESTION:
Enjoy with Fever-Tree Premium Indian Tonic Water.

Waitoki Washhouse

Waitoki Washhouse Gin

43% ABV

A modern dry style gin, Waitoki Washhouse Gin was born out of 40 different recipes over the course of 18 months, combining traditional botanicals with native kawakawa and horopito, fresh orange and grapefruit, and additions from a local tree that is 200+ years old.

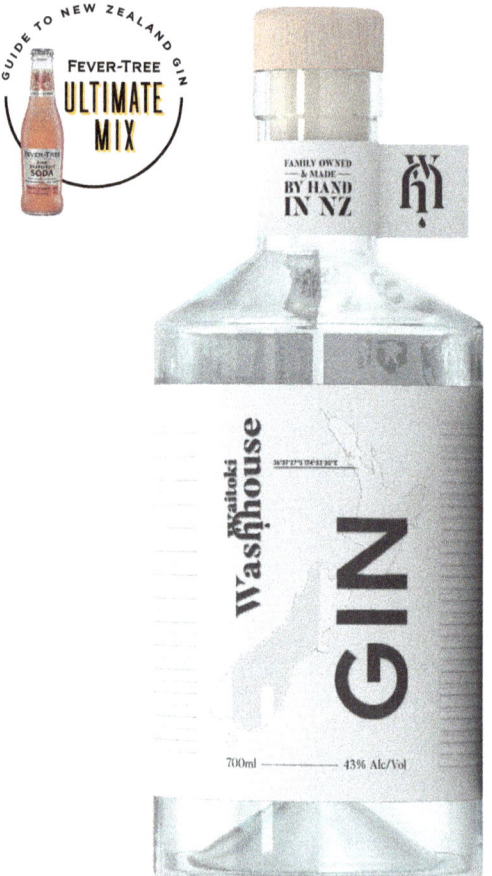

DISTILLERY:
Washhouse Distillery, Waitoki

BOTANICALS:
Juniper, Coriander Seed, Angelica Root, Orange, Grapefruit, Kawakawa, Horopito & Others

TASTING NOTES:
Grapefruit peel and native green leaf on the nose, orange sweetness with root spice and pronounced peppery heat on the palate, drying pepper and kawakawa to finish.

SERVING SUGGESTION:
Enjoy with Fever-Tree Aromatic Tonic Water.

Yen Gin
42% ABV

A modern dry style gin, Yen Gin was developed by an award-winning mixologist to be a balanced drink using locally foraged botanicals and is the world's first NFT tokenized gin.

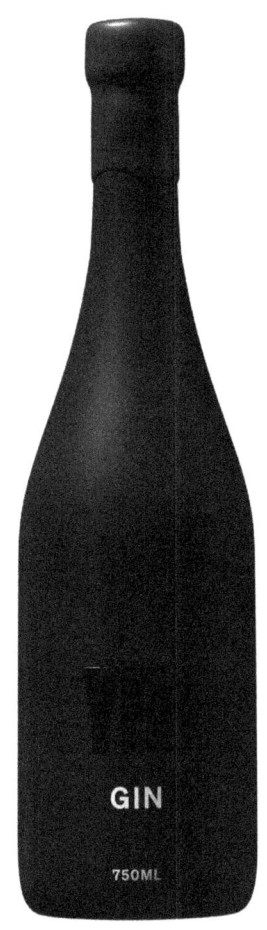

DISTILLERY:
The Spirits Workshop, Christchurch

BOTANICALS:
Juniper, Pink Peppercorn, Orange, Liquorice & Kawakawa

TASTING NOTES:
Peppercorn and orange sherbet with kawakawa undertones on the nose, kawakawa and orange lead with pink peppercorn on the palate, sweet liquorice and orange to finish.

SERVING SUGGESTION:
Enjoy with Fever-Tree Premium Indian Tonic Water.

CONTEMPORARY

CONTEMPORARY

Gins with modern, new world and/or local botanical flavour that is more prominent than juniper.

Ariki Ultra Premium Gin
45% ABV

A contemporary gin, Ariki Ultra Premium Gin is a smooth collaboration of pure New Zealand water and unique Pacific botanicals including Rarotongan vanilla and Tongan coconut.

DISTILLERY:
Ariki Spirit, Mount Maunganui

BOTANICALS:
Juniper, Almond, Coriander Seed, Angelica Root, Orange Peel, Orris Root, Lemon Peel, Liquorice, Black Peppercorn, Cardamom, Manuka Flower, Cinnamon, Lemon Grass, Vanilla & Coconut

TASTING NOTES:
Coconut, vanilla and marzipan on the nose, creamy and sweet orange with coconut, vanilla and marzipan on the palate, black pepper leads a quick finish.

SERVING SUGGESTION:
Enjoy with Fever-Tree Refreshingly Light Indian Tonic Water.

Awildian Coromandel Dry Gin

47% ABV

A contemporary gin, Awildian Coromandel Dry Gin is made using 20 botanicals and water from the Coromandel Ranges and rested for three weeks before a final reduction to its bottling strength of 47% ABV.

DISTILLERY:
Coromandel Distilling Co., Thames

BOTANICALS:
Juniper, Coriander Seed, Angelica Root, Seville Orange, Lemon Thyme, Hibiscus, Blueberry, Lemon Myrtle, Rose Petal, Cubeb & Others

TASTING NOTES:
Complex florals and earthy tones with coriander and citrus on the nose, delicate florals, peppercorn and orange accented by subtle juniper on the palate, soft florals and herbal undertones to finish.

SERVING SUGGESTION:
Enjoy with Fever-Tree Mediterranean Tonic Water.

Awildian Coromandel Dry Gin - Blue Edition

47% ABV

A contemporary gin, Awildian Coromandel Dry Gin Blue Edition uses their Coromandel Dry Gin as its base with the addition of Butterfly Pea Flowers which gives it its rich purple blue colour.

DISTILLERY:
Coromandel Distilling Co., Thames

BOTANICALS:
Juniper, Coriander Seed, Angelica Root, Seville Orange, Lemon Thyme, Hibiscus, Blueberry, Lemon Myrtle, Rose Petal, Cubeb, Butterfly Pea Flower & Others.

TASTING NOTES:
Complex florals and earthy tones with vibrant coriander and citrus on the nose, delicate florals, peppercorn and orange accented by subtle juniper on the palate, slight bitterness to finish.

SERVING SUGGESTION:
Enjoy with Fever-Tree Mediterranean Tonic Water.

Awildian Coromandel Spiced Gin

47% ABV

A contemporary Gin, Awildian Coromandel Spiced Gin is made using 23 botanicals, the majority of which are spices, with a 16 hour maceration and blended with water from the Coromandel Ranges after distillation.

DISTILLERY:
Coromandel Distilling Co., Thames

BOTANICALS:
Juniper, Coriander, Ginger, Angelica, Cardamom, Cubeb, Cassia, Ceylon Cinnamon, Lavender, Fennel, Chamomile, Seville Orange, Lime, Nutmeg, Star Anise, Aniseed & Others

TASTING NOTES:
Ginger root, aniseed and strong green pepper on the nose, hot and peppery with bold aniseed and baking spice on the palate, aniseed and heat carry with liquorice to finish.

SERVING SUGGESTION:
Enjoy with Fever-Tree Ginger Ale.

The Bureaucrat

41% ABV

A contemporary gin, Bureaucrats Gin The Bureaucrat Gin has a combination of ten botanicals with bold flavours of spice and sweet undertones.

DISTILLERY:
Bureaucrats Gin Ltd., Wellington

BOTANICALS:
Juniper, Coriander Seed, Cinnamon & Others

TASTING NOTES:
Pronounced baking spice with ginger on the nose, off dry sweetness driven by cinnamon and ginger on the palate, coriander and cinnamon lead a slightly bitter finish.

SERVING SUGGESTION:
Enjoy with Fever-Tree Aromatic Tonic Water.

The Doyenne
41% ABV

A contemporary gin, Bureaucrats The Doyenne Gin uses a unique combination of botanicals, including coconut, lime, and zesty lemongrass.

DISTILLERY:
Bureaucrats Gin Ltd., Wellington

BOTANICALS:
Juniper, Coriander Seed, Coconut, Lime, Lemongrass & Others

TASTING NOTES:
Savoury lemongrass with lime on the nose, soft coconut creaminess, fresh coriander and lime fuse on the palate, a long lime driven finish.

SERVING SUGGESTION:
Enjoy with Fever-Tree Mediterranean Tonic Water.

The Cambridge Distillery Company

Knocknaveagh Cambridge Dry Gin
41% ABV

A contemporary gin, Knocknaveagh Cambridge Dry Gin was conceived as the counterpoint to a London Dry, with a nod to tradition but a twist of modernity.

DISTILLERY:
The Cambridge Distillery Company, Cambridge

BOTANICALS:
Juniper, Coriander Seed, Angelica Root, Cardamom, Grapefruit, Chamomile, Black Peppercorn & Douglas Fir

TASTING NOTES:
Complex fruits, brewed chamomile tea and a touch of dry straw on the nose, chamomile leads with grapefruit flesh on the palate, developing cardamom and angelica to finish.

SERVING SUGGESTION:
Enjoy with Fever-Tree Refreshingly Light Indian Tonic Water.

Curiosity Gin - Recipe #23

42% ABV

A contemporary gin, Curiosity Gin Recipe #23 is made using a base spirit distilled in-house from Canterbury malted barley and 11 botanicals including a generous helping of East Coast Manuka, fresh citrus, and Otago lavender.

DISTILLERY:
The Spirits Workshop Distillery, Christchurch

BOTANICALS:
Juniper, Manuka Berry, Manuka Leaf, Coriander Seed, Cardamom, Orange Zest, Lime Zest, Ginger, Angelica Root, Lavender, Cinnamon & Star Anise

TASTING NOTES:
Gentle pine, coriander and sweet herbs lead the nose, delicate spice, zesty citrus and light juniper on the palate, ginger and anise lingering to finish.

SERVING SUGGESTION:
Enjoy with Fever-Tree Refreshingly Light Indian Tonic Water.

Coatsvillien Spice Gin 2022 Harvest
41% ABV

A contemporary gin, Coatesvillian Spice Gin 2022 Harvest is a limited release that celebrates rural Coatesville and its gardens by using botanicals foraged from local private gardens.

DISTILLERY:
D.Still Project, Coatesville

BOTANICALS:
Juniper, Coriander Seed, Angelica Root, Orange, Cassia, Cardamom, Pimento, Ginger, Liquorice & Almond

TASTING NOTES:
Cassia, ginger and cardamom lead the nose, peppery juniper with tart citrus and spicy ginger on the palate, cardamom and ginger lead a warming finish.

SERVING SUGGESTION:
Enjoy with Fever-Tree Aromatic Tonic Water.

Denzien Distiller's Proof #15 Teatree

41% ABV

A contemporary gin, Denzien Distiller's Proof #15 Teatree came from the idea of creating a 'Breakfast' gin, with a long process of tasting different tea varieties and combinations to create the right blend for gin.

DISTILLERY:
Denzien Urban Distillery, Wellington

BOTANICALS:
Juniper, Coriander Seed, Fennel Seed, Angelica Root, Orris Root, Manuka Leaf, Black Tea, Bergamot Oil, Lemon Peel, Lemongrass & Blue Cornflower Blossom

TASTING NOTES:
Deep earth, fennel and black tea on the nose, dark liquorice and fennel with a juniper and earthy root backbone on the palate, lingering dark earth and juniper to finish.

SERVING SUGGESTION:
Enjoy with Fever-Tree Aromatic Tonic Water.

Denzien Smoke & Embers Gin

44% ABV

A contemporary gin, Denzien Smoke & Embers Gin is designed to mimic some of the qualities of whiskey by including Morita, chipotle, and habanero as botanicals.

DISTILLERY:
Denzien Urban Distillery, Wellington

BOTANICALS:
Juniper, Morita Chilli, Chipotle, Guajillo Chilli, California Chilli, Mulato Negro Chilli, Habanero Chilli, Coriander Seed, Angelica Root, Fennel Seed, Liquorice & Orris Root

TASTING NOTES:
Delicate smoke and light chilli on the nose, subtle pepper, fennel and root spice on the palate, aniseed gently drives the finish.

SERVING SUGGESTION:
Enjoy with Fever-Tree Ginger Ale.

Dr Beak

Dr Beak Garden Gin

45.5% ABV

A contemporary gin, Dr Beak New Zealand Garden Gin was designed around their seven core botanicals to be fresh and sprightly like the Piwakawaka, or fantail.

DISTILLERY:
Arise Spirits, Martinborough

BOTANICALS:
Juniper, Coriander Seed, Orris Root, Horopito, Rosemary, Mint & Bay Leaf

TASTING NOTES:
Fresh green herbs, juniper and mint lead the nose, savoury herbs lead with a bright mintiness on the palate, a long dry juniper driven finish.

SERVING SUGGESTION:
Enjoy with Fever-Tree Mediterranean Tonic Water.

ULTIMATE MIX
GIMLET

Dr Beak

Dr Beak Yuzu Garden Gin

45.5% ABV

A contemporary gin, Dr Beak Yuzu Garden Gin is a limited release version of their New Zealand Garden Gin with the addition of fresh, locally grown yuzu.

DISTILLERY:
Arise Spirits, Martinborough

BOTANICALS:
Juniper, Coriander Seed, Orris Root, Horopito, Rosemary, Mint, Bay Leaf & Yuzu

TASTING NOTES:
Juniper, yuzu flesh, and bold mint lead the nose, yuzu flesh leads with lingering juniper and horopito heat on the palate, lingering bay leaf and rosemary to the finish.

SERVING SUGGESTION:
Enjoy with Fever-Tree Mediterranean Tonic Water.

Dr Beak

Dr Beak New Zealand Premium Gin
48% ABV

A contemporary gin, Dr Beak New Zealand Premium Gin is bursting with flavour due to the high number of essential oils and will proudly cloud up when left in the freezer or mixed with tonic.

DISTILLERY:
Arise Spirits, Martinborough

BOTANICALS:
Juniper, Coriander Seed, Lavender, Mint, Chamomile, Lemon Verbena, Orris Root, Thyme, Rosemary, Lime Peel, Kelp, Horopito & Bay Leaf

TASTING NOTES:
Herbaceous greens, damp mint, and a slight dry grass character on the nose, pronounced garden herbs lead with lime and root spice on the palate, an earthy bay driven finish.

SERVING SUGGESTION:
Enjoy with Fever-Tree Mediterranean Tonic Water.

Dunedin Craft Distillers Dunedin Dry Gin

40% ABV

A contemporary gin, Dunedin Craft Distillers Dunedin Dry Gin was made to be an accessible sipping gin or a versatile mixer using their own base spirit, fermented from surplus bread and bakery products.

DISTILLERY:
Dunedin Craft Distillers, Dunedin

BOTANICALS:
Juniper, Coriander Seed, Angelica Root, Liquorice, Cassia, Orris Root & Lemon

TASTING NOTES:
Characterful base notes with hints of tropical fruit on the nose, cassia, lemon and liquorice on the palate, drying light spice leads the finish.

SERVING SUGGESTION:
Enjoy with Fever-Tree Premium Indian Tonic Water.

Dunedin Craft Distillers The Bay
48% ABV

A contemporary gin, Dunedin Craft Distillers The Bay Gin is a limited release in their 'Working Titles' series designed to be a back to basics gin with citrus and herbal notes.

DISTILLERY:
Dunedin Craft Distillers, Dunedin

BOTANICALS:
Juniper, Coriander Seed, Bay Leaf & Lemon

TASTING NOTES:
Base notes provide a sweet fruitiness with waxy bay undertones on the nose, light juniper bolstered by coriander and bay on the palate, developing florals and sweet citrus to finish.

SERVING SUGGESTION:
Enjoy with Fever-Tree Mediterranean Tonic Water.

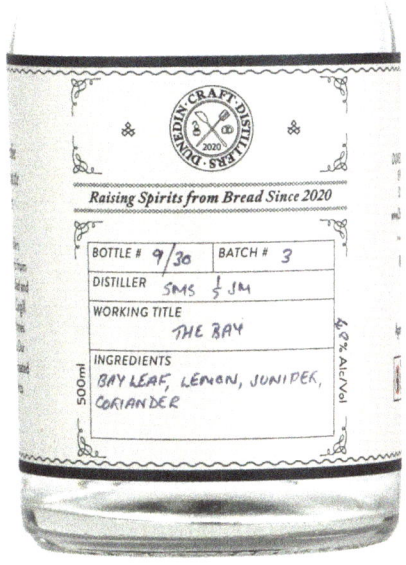

ELSEWHERE

TRIPLE GIN — HAND CRAFTED

Elsewhere Endeavour Inlet Triple Gin

42% ABV

A contemporary gin, Elsewhere Endeavour Inlet Triple Gin is a limited edition that takes inspiration from the area that it is named after in the Queen Charlotte Sound, and where many of its botanicals are sourced, with a pale golden colour.

DISTILLERY:
Elsewhere Gin, Christchurch

BOTANICALS:
Juniper, Coriander Seed, Angelica Root, Mandarin Zest, Grapefruit, Cardamom, Rata Flower, Rimu Frond, Honeysuckle Enfleurage, Fennel Blossom, Wakame Seaweed & Mafic Metavolcanic Marine Rock

TASTING NOTES:
Juicy grapefruit and mandarin with pine undertones on the nose, soft mandarin with supporting spice, developing blossoms and a light minerality on the palate, warming citrus peel mellows to finish.

SERVING SUGGESTION:
Enjoy with Fever-Tree Premium Indian Tonic Water.

ELSEWHERE
TRIPLE GIN — HAND CRAFTED

Elsewhere Hahei Triple Gin
42% ABV

A contemporary gin, Elsewhere Hahei Triple Gin is made with freshly foraged botanicals from Hahei to express a strong sense of nostalgia, with a delicate pink colour.

DISTILLERY:
Elsewhere Gin, Christchurch

BOTANICALS:
Juniper, Coriander Seed, Angelica Root, Nutmeg, Cardamom, Tarata Resin, Manuka Blossom, Sea Lettuce, Kawakawa Fruit, Makrut Lime, Kumquat & Ignimbrite

TASTING NOTES:
Soft makrut, juicy citrus and a salt water spray on the nose, fruity makrut and kawakawa notes held together by a resin backbone on the palate, drying citrus and gentle nutmeg to finish.

SERVING SUGGESTION:
Enjoy with Fever-Tree Mediterranean Tonic Water.

GUIDE TO NEW ZEALAND GIN — VOL. 3 — HIGHLY COMMENDED

GUIDE TO NEW ZEALAND GIN — ULTIMATE MIX — DIRTY MARTINI

ELSEWHERE

TRIPLE GIN — HAND CRAFTED

Elsewhere Little River Triple Gin

42% ABV

A contemporary gin, Elsewhere Little River Triple Gin is made with butterfly pea flower to give it a bright, dusty blue colour that becomes the lavender blush of early mornings at Birdling's Flat when mixed with tonic.

GUIDE TO NEW ZEALAND GIN — VOL. 3 — HIGHLY COMMENDED

DISTILLERY:
Elsewhere Gin, Christchurch

BOTANICALS:
Juniper, Coriander Seed, Angelica Root, Nutmeg, Liquorice, Lemon Peel, Butterfly Pea Flower, Chamomile, Lemon Thyme, Lemon Verbena, Rosemary, Tarata Blossom, Kombu & Beach Agate

TASTING NOTES:
Delicate florals, light citrus and umami undertones on the nose, juniper and light pine with an array of florals and lemon verbena backbone on the palate, flavours continue to develop alongside liquorice to finish.

SERVING SUGGESTION:
Enjoy with Fever-Tree Refreshingly Light Indian Tonic Water.

ELSEWHERE
TRIPLE GIN — HAND CRAFTED

Elsewhere + Austin Club Little Akaloa Triple Gin
42% ABV

A contemporary gin, Elsewhere + Austin Club Little Akaloa Triple Gin is made with botanicals foraged from Little Akaloa, with the help of the Austin Club, to capture the Banks Peninsula landscape.

DISTILLERY:
Elsewhere Gin, Christchurch

BOTANICALS:
Juniper, Coriander Seed, Angelica Root, Cinnamon, Cassia, Horopito Peppercorn, Kohia (Native Passionfruit), Kawakawa, Kombu & Yuzu

TASTING NOTES:
Tart passionfruit, dusted cinnamon and herbal undertones on the nose, soft passionfruit with bitter herbs and peppery heat on the palate, dried apricot character with warming spice to finish.

SERVING SUGGESTION:
Enjoy with Fever-Tree Refreshingly Light Indian Tonic Water.

1564 Venus & Adonis Shakespeare's Gin

40% ABV

A contemporary gin, Fenton Street Gin 1564 Venus & Adonis Shakespeare's Gin is named for the poet's most popular poem with botanicals selected to represent each of the lovers and their story.

DISTILLERY:
Fenton Street Distillery, Stratford

BOTANICALS:
Juniper, Dandelion Root, Rose Petal, Rimu, Coriander Seed, Citrus, Angelica Root, Kawakawa & Miro Berry

TASTING NOTES:
Piny resinous green wood and kawakawa on the nose, pepper spice, native notes and bitter roots drive the palate, leading to a heated spice driven finish.

SERVING SUGGESTION:
Enjoy with Fever-Tree Mediterranean Tonic Water.

The Artist

40% ABV

A contemporary gin, Fenton Street Gin The Artist is triple distilled with horopito and ginger alongside a range of other botanicals to produce a gin that appeals to whiskey drinkers.

DISTILLERY:
Fenton Street Distillery, Stratford

BOTANICALS:
Juniper, Coriander Seed, Cassia, Nutmeg, Ginger, Horopito, Pepper & Kawakawa

TASTING NOTES:
Ginger, horopito pepper and green kawakawa on the nose, pronounced green spice and lemon with native notes carrying on the palate, heat driven bitter finish.

SERVING SUGGESTION:
Enjoy with Fever-Tree Mediterranean Tonic Water.

The Beast with Two Backs
40% ABV

A contemporary gin, Fenton Street Gin The Beast with Two Backs is designed to reflect the love of Othello, represented by cassia and coffee beans among others, and Desdemona, represented by Pohutukawa, in Shakespeare's Othello.

DISTILLERY:
Fenton Street Distillery, Stratford

BOTANICALS:
Juniper, Pohutukawa Stamen, Caramelised Orange, Nutmeg, Cassia, Turmeric, Liquorice & Coffee Bean

TASTING NOTES:
Classic baking spice with green earthiness and hints of bitter spice on the nose, light spice and earthy characters continue on the palate, developing pepper with earthy florals to finish.

SERVING SUGGESTION:
Enjoy with Fever-Tree Mediterranean Tonic Water.

The Novelist
40% ABV

A contemporary gin, Fenton Street Gin The Novelist uses bush honey from eastern Taranaki to draw together its other botanicals into a smooth yet complex gin.

DISTILLERY:
Fenton Street Distillery, Stratford

BOTANICALS:
Juniper, Angelica Root, Coriander Seed, Horopito, Cassia, Bush Honey, Orris Root, Almond, Liquorice & Lime

TASTING NOTES:
Honey and horopito on the nose, nutty spice, vibrant lime and horopito pepper on the palate, liquorice sweetness develops to finish.

SERVING SUGGESTION:
Enjoy with Fever-Tree Premium Indian Tonic Water.

The Poet
40% ABV

A contemporary gin, Fenton Street Gin The Poet is designed to celebrate the traditional character of a London Dry gin and capture a simple expression of summer with the inclusion of New Zealand citruses.

DISTILLERY:
Fenton Street Distillery, Stratford

BOTANICALS:
Juniper, Coriander Seed, Angelica Root, Orange Zest, Lime Zest, Cardamom & Orris Root

TASTING NOTES:
Cardamom, root spice and soft florals on the nose, citrus zest and green spice drive the palate, a warming green spice finish.

SERVING SUGGESTION:
Enjoy with Fever-Tree Premium Indian Tonic Water.

The Vintner
46% ABV

A contemporary gin, Fenton Street Gin The Vintner showcases tannins from oak staves that are immersed in red wine for 24 months before distillation.

DISTILLERY:
Fenton Street Distillery, Stratford

BOTANICALS:
Juniper, Coriander Seed, Tarata, Horopito, Nutmeg, Oak Staves, Lemon Zest, Cassia, Peppercorn, Bush Honey, Angelica Root & Kawakawa

TASTING NOTES:
Oak dominant with hints of piny juniper on the nose, root spice, honey and native herbs on the palate, a long and rich oak driven finish.

SERVING SUGGESTION:
Enjoy with Fever-Tree Premium Indian Tonic Water.

Grey Lynn Gin Parma Violet
37.5% ABV

A contemporary gin, Grey Lynn Parma Violet is made with minimal botanicals to uphold their approach to creating bold and uncompromising tastes.

DISTILLERY:
Grey Lynn Gin, Auckland

BOTANICALS:
Juniper, Apple, Cardamom & Lavender

TASTING NOTES:
Lavender and cardamom on the nose, baked apple and sea salt caramel on the palate, a touch of floral sweetness to finish.

SERVING SUGGESTION:
Enjoy with Fever-Tree Elderflower Tonic Water.

Grey Lynn Gin Signature Citrus
37.5% ABV

A contemporary gin, Grey Lynn Gin Signature Citrus came about as the result of an intense trial and error process and includes a secret local ingredient.

DISTILLERY:
Grey Lynn Gin, Auckland

BOTANICALS:
Juniper, Orange Peel, Fennel Seed & Lemon Peel

TASTING NOTES:
Overripe orange and fennel on the nose, strong lemon and juniper on the palate, slightly chalky, bitter herb finish.

SERVING SUGGESTION:
Enjoy with Fever-Tree Premium Indian Tonic Water.

Albertine Gin
47% ABV

A contemporary gin, Hastings Distillers Albertine Gin contains 38 organic botanicals with the goal of creating a sensory landscape of the freshness and vibrancy of New Zealand.

VOL. 3 — HIGHLY COMMENDED

2021 — TASTERS' PICK

DISTILLERY:
Hastings Distillers, Hastings

BOTANICALS:
Juniper, Coriander Seed, Angelica Root, Lime Peel, Lemon Peel, Orange Peel, Makrut Lime Leaf, Makrut Lime Peel, Grapefruit Peel, Lemon Verbena, Lemongrass, Lavender, Chamomile, Manuka Flower, Sage, Rosemary, Mace & Others

TASTING NOTES:
Fragrant chamomile, green bush flowers and waxy citrus zest on the nose, pronounced makrut lime, angelica and savoury herbs on the palate, lingering mace and fresh pepper heat to finish.

SERVING SUGGESTION:
Enjoy with Fever-Tree Mediterranean Tonic Water.

Autumn Gin
40% ABV

A contemporary gin, Hastings Distillers Autumn Gin is a limited edition perfumed and spiced with nine organic botanicals to convey the fragrance of the Hawke's Bay harvest.

DISTILLERY:
Hastings Distillers, Hastings

BOTANICALS:
Juniper, Encore Mandarin Peel, Encore Mandarin Fruit, Quince, Feijoa Leaf, Lemongrass, Tarragon, Cassia & Lemon Verbena

TASTING NOTES:
Juicy mandarin with blossoming floral notes on the nose, upfront mandarin with a touch of tarragon and waxy lemongrass on the palate, pleasant mandarin flesh to finish.

SERVING SUGGESTION:
Enjoy with Fever-Tree Mediterranean Tonic Water.

Blossom Parade Gin

42% ABV

A contemporary gin, Hastings Distillers Blossom Parade Gin is a limited edition designed to capture the fleeting scents of spring with its floral and perfumed botanicals.

DISTILLERY:
Hastings Distillers, Hastings

BOTANICALS:
Juniper, Orange Blossom, Confetti Bush, Lemon Myrtle, Lavender, Rose Root, Allspice & Lemon Peel

TASTING NOTES:
Bold lemon myrtle bolstered by floral blossoms on the nose, lemon myrtle leads with strong floral tones and a hint of allspice on the palate, lavender and sweet lemon to finish.

SERVING SUGGESTION:
Enjoy with Fever-Tree Elderflower Tonic Water.

East Block 200

40% ABV

A contemporary dry style gin, Hastings Distillers East Block 200 Gin is an unconventional interpretation of a London Dry containing ten organic botanicals, eight of which are grown in Hawke's Bay.

DISTILLERY:
Hastings Distillers, Hastings

BOTANICALS:
Juniper, Coriander Seed, Angelica Root, Orange Peel, Lemon Peel, Makrut Lime Peel, Cassia, Feijoa Leaf, Bay Leaf & Lavender

TASTING NOTES:
Complex green waxy leaves with citrus peel and soft juniper on the nose, bold makrut lime, sweet citrus and bitter juniper on the palate, building citrus and angelica to finish.

SERVING SUGGESTION:
Enjoy with Fever-Tree Mediterranean Tonic Water.

Hector's Long Harbour Ocean Wash Gin
42% ABV

A contemporary gin, Hector's Long Harbour Ocean Wash Gin is named for the Hector's dolphins that swim off of Akaroa and takes its flavour profile from botanicals foraged around Banks Peninsula blended wth classic botanicals.

DISTILLERY:
Akaroa Craft Distillery, Akaroa

BOTANICALS:
Juniper, Kelp, Manuka, Thyme, Lemon Myrtle, Orange, Lavender, Cardamom, Cinnamon, Angelica Root, Orris Root, Liquorice & Coriander Seed

TASTING NOTES:
Bold lemon myrtle and cardamom with a subtle sea breeze on the nose, lemon myrtle, cardamom and orris on the palate, confectionary-like lemon sweetness to finish.

SERVING SUGGESTION:
Enjoy with Fever-Tree Mediterranean Tonic Water.

imagination Wakame Seaweed Dry Gin
42% ABV

A contemporary gin, imagination New Zealand Wakame Seaweed Dry Gin is made using wild wakame seaweed, known for its saltiness and umami flavour, foraged from the Wellington and Wairarapa coasts.

DISTILLERY:
imagination, Reikorangi

BOTANICALS:
Juniper, Coriander Seed, Lime, Orange, Lemon, Cassia, Liquorice, Green Cardamom, Orris Root & Wakame Seaweed

TASTING NOTES:
Citrus peel, root spice and subtle juniper lead the nose, green cardamom, liquorice root and soft juniper are accented by a saltiness on the palate, warming spice to finish.

SERVING SUGGESTION:
Enjoy with Fever-Tree Lime & Yuzu Soda.

Island Gin Original

43.2% ABV

A contemporary dry style gin, Island Gin Original is focused on the inclusion of both Manuka and bush honey from Great Barrier Island along with other special island flora.

GUIDE TO NEW ZEALAND GIN — VOL. 3 — HIGHLY COMMENDED

GUIDE TO NEW ZEALAND GIN — FEVER-TREE ULTIMATE MIX

DISTILLERY:
Island Gin Distillery, Great Barrier

BOTANICALS:
Juniper, Manuka Honey, Bush Honey, Coriander Seed, Lemon Myrtle & Others

TASTING NOTES:
Vibrant green herbs, coriander and bitter lemon on the nose, upfront citrus with peppery herbs accented by a subtle juniper and coriander on the palate, warming earthy spice to finish.

SERVING SUGGESTION:
Enjoy with Fever-Tree Refreshingly Light Indian Tonic Water.

Juniper Jinn
40% ABV

A contemporary gin, Juniper Distillery Juniper Jinn is their signature gin made in a London Dry style with lots of juniper and sealed with red wax.

DISTILLERY:
Juniper Distillery, Rangiora

BOTANICALS:
Juniper, Lavender & Lemon

TASTING NOTES:
Pronounced grain tones on the nose, malty tones continue with hints of juniper on the palate, strong cereal driven finish.

SERVING SUGGESTION:
Enjoy with Fever-Tree Premium Indian Tonic Water.

Juno Autumn 2022

44% ABV

A contemporary gin, Juno Autumn 2022 Seasonal Gin evokes autumn with a combination of flavours from New Zealand coastal forest and the sea, featuring artwork by Jessica Rozencwajg on the bottle.

DISTILLERY:
Begin Distilling, New Plymouth

BOTANICALS:
Juniper, Coriander Seed, Angelica Root, Orris Root, Cassia, Orange, Cardamom, Nutmeg, Flax, Manuka, Kawakawa, Horopito, Manuka, Kauri, Wakame Seaweed, Lavender & Lemon

TASTING NOTES:
Savoury seaweed, kawakawa and zingy lemon on the nose, horopito pepper with baking spice and bitter forest floor elements on the palate, lavender and lemon to finish.

SERVING SUGGESTION:
Enjoy with Fever-Tree Mediterranean Tonic Water.

JUNO GIN

Juno Winter 2022

44% ABV

A contemporary gin, Juno Winter 2022 Seasonal Gin is inspired by a Three Sisters Brewery and Small Gods Brewery collaboration, nicknamed Winter Weeds Gin and featuring artwork by Hiroaki Teraoka on the bottle.

DISTILLERY:
Begin Distilling, New Plymouth

BOTANICALS:
Juniper, Coriander Seed, Angelica Root, Orris Root, Cassia, Orange, Cardamom, Nutmeg, Dandelion Root, Burdock, Smoked Gorse & Meadowsweet

TASTING NOTES:
Musky earth, light spice and a hay-like note on the nose, nutmeg leads with supporting juniper, mild orange and orris on the palate, building coriander and warming spice to finish.

SERVING SUGGESTION:
Enjoy with Fever-Tree Aromatic Tonic Water.

Agatha's Tears Dark Gin

42% ABV

A contemporary gin, Agatha's Tears Dark Gin celebrates the Waikino Hotel's resident spirit, a former madam of the house who wanders the halls with her young friend, Emily, who is the cause of her tears, with a dark blue colour.

DISTILLERY:
Kaimai Brewing & Distilling Co., Waikino

BOTANICALS:
Juniper, Cardamom, Cubeb, Coriander Seed, Cinnamon, Angelica Root & Ginger

TASTING NOTES:
Cardamom and cinnamon dominate the nose, bold cardamom and cinnamon continue with sharp ginger and juniper on the palate, peppery heat with lasting cardamom to finish.

SERVING SUGGESTION:
Enjoy with Fever-Tree Aromatic Tonic Water.

Eliza's Claim Dry Gin
47% ABV

A contemporary gin, Eliza's Claim Dry Gin is named in memory of a pioneering goldmine in the Kaimai Ranges with gold flakes to reflect the heritage of the area where it is made.

DISTILLERY:
Kaimai Brewing & Distilling Co., Waikino

BOTANICALS:
Juniper, Angelica Root, Rosemary, Manuka Honey & Others

TASTING NOTES:
Bold rosemary and honey on the nose, savoury heat opens with oily rosemary and juicy herbs continuing on the palate, a lingering spicy finish.

SERVING SUGGESTION:
Enjoy with Fever-Tree Mediterranean Tonic Water.

Eliza's Claim Gold Gin
47% ABV

A contemporary gin, Eliza's Claim Gold Gin combines 12 botanicals with 50,000-year-old water from an artesian aquifer in the Coromandel Ranges and gold flakes resulting in a pale golden colour.

DISTILLERY:
Kaimai Brewing & Distilling Co., Waikino

BOTANICALS:
Juniper, Angelica Root, Rosemary, Manuka Honey & Others

TASTING NOTES:
Soft florals, herbaceous flowers and honey on the nose, sweet green herbs lead with a distinct honey character on the palate, warming herbs to finish.

SERVING SUGGESTION:
Enjoy with Fever-Tree Mediterranean Tonic Water.

Sirius' Find Truffle Gin

47% ABV

A contemporary gin, Sirius' Find Truffle Gin was created as a celebration of the New Zealand truffle industry, infused with Périgord black truffles and complementary herbs.

DISTILLERY:
Kaimai Brewing & Distilling Co., Waikino

BOTANICALS:
Juniper, Périgord Black Truffle, Sage, Thyme, Basil, Rosemary, Oregano, Angelica Root & Horopito

TASTING NOTES:
Musty mushroom, horopito pepper, and garden herbs on the nose, herbal-forward with thyme, basil and sage dominating the palate, lingering culinary herbs to finish.

SERVING SUGGESTION:
Enjoy with Fever-Tree Mediterranean Tonic Water.

Kākāpō Kawakawa and Pink Peppercorn Gin

42% ABV

A contemporary gin, Kakapo Kawakawa and Pink Peppercorn Gin is made using kawakawa handpicked from their property and pink peppercorn picked in its native home of Peru.

DISTILLERY:
Kakapo Distillery, Whangaparaoa

BOTANICALS:
Juniper, Coriander Seed, Kawakawa, Pink Peppercorn, Orris Root, Rosehip, Lime Peel, Cardamom & Liquorice

TASTING NOTES:
Strong pink peppercorn with hints of green herbs on the nose, bold pepper with a touch of kawakawa on the palate, very strong heat to finish.

SERVING SUGGESTION:
Enjoy with Fever-Tree Premium Indian Tonic Water.

Kākāpō Mānuka Honey and Elderflower Gin
42% ABV

A contemporary gin, Kakapo Manuka Honey and Elderflower Gin is made using Manuka honey sustainably sourced from Great Barrier Island, with a certified MGO rating of 125+, and wild Otago elderflower.

DISTILLERY:
Kakapo Distillery, Whangaparaoa

BOTANICALS:
Juniper, Coriander Seed, Manuka Honey, Elderflower, Manuka, Rosehip, Lavender, Orris Root, Lime Peel & Lemon Verbena

TASTING NOTES:
Rounded honey and sweet herbs with subtle juniper on the nose, lemon verbena and musky lavender with hints of soft honey on the palate, lingering heat with mild juniper to finish.

SERVING SUGGESTION:
Enjoy with Fever-Tree Elderflower Tonic Water.

Katipō Aotearoa Dry Gin

44% ABV

A contemporary gin, Katipo Aotearoa Dry Gin is a classic Kiwi take on a traditional London Dry, introducing Nelson Sauvin hops to its otherwise classic botanicals.

DISTILLERY:
Kakapo Distilling Co., Napier

BOTANICALS:
Juniper, Lemon, Nelson Sauvin Hop, Orris Root, Angelica Root, Liquorice, Cassia & Cardamom

TASTING NOTES:
Freshly baked cassia with funky hop notes on the nose, cassia continues with resinous juniper and spicy cardamom on the palate, angelica and liquorice carry into the finish.

SERVING SUGGESTION:
Enjoy with Fever-Tree Premium Indian Tonic Water.

1963 Butterfly Pea Flower Gin
43% ABV

A contemporary gin, 1963 Butterfly Pea Flower Gin is a blend of their Premium Dry Gin with the addition of butterfly pea flower which imparts a deep blue colour that changes when mixed with tonic.

DISTILLERY:
Kim Crawford Distillery, Cromwell

BOTANICALS:
Juniper, Coriander Seed, Lemon Peel, Orange Peel, Star Anise, Fennel Seed, Butterfly Pea Flower & Cinnamon

TASTING NOTES:
Powdered cinnamon and star anise dominate the nose, liquorice, strong star anise and cinnamon on the palate, earthy spice and lingering fennel to finish.

SERVING SUGGESTION:
Enjoy with Fever-Tree Aromatic Tonic Water.

KIWI SPIRIT DISTILLERY

Greenstone Gin
40% ABV

A contemporary gin, Greenstone Gin is a blend of tradition and new ideas including native totara and kahikatea botanicals twice distilled with pure water from the nearby Te Waikoropupu Springs.

DISTILLERY:
Kiwi Spirits Distillery, Motupipi

BOTANICALS:
Juniper, Totara, Kahikatea & Others

TASTING NOTES:
Striking ginger and root spice on the nose, sweet hints of liquorice with forest floor elements on the palate, lingering baking spice and pine to finish.

SERVING SUGGESTION:
Enjoy with Fever-Tree Refreshingly Light Indian Tonic Water.

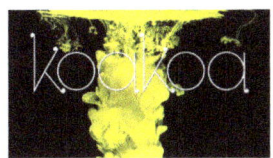

Koakoa Tīni Rēmana Gin
41% ABV

A contemporary gin, Koakoa Tini Remana Gin is inspired by New Zealand's history of making lemon based treats and the Italian lemon liqueur limoncello.

DISTILLERY:
Koakoa, Paraparaumu Beach

BOTANICALS:
Juniper & Others

TASTING NOTES:
Lemon myrtle and menthol spice on the nose, orange and lemon peel lead with a touch of Manuka honey sweetness on the palate, citrus drives a quick finish.

SERVING SUGGESTION:
Enjoy with Fever-Tree Refreshingly Light Indian Tonic Water.

The Bond Store Kawakawa Gin
37.5% ABV

A contemporary gin, The Bond Store Kawakawa Gin is made using a unique selection of botanicals including kawakawa grown on the family farm in rural Wairarapa.

DISTILLERY:
Koakoa, Paraparaumu

BOTANICALS:
Juniper, Kawakawa & Others

TASTING NOTES:
Kawakawa, citrus and faint cinnamon on the nose, candy-sweet lemon, herbaceous kawakawa and pepper heat on the palate, dry spice driven finish.

SERVING SUGGESTION:
Enjoy with Fever-Tree Mediterranean Tonic Water.

Lady H Artisan New Zealand Gin

42% ABV

A contemporary gin, Lady H Artisan New Zealand Gin is made with botanicals selected for their delicate aromas and fresh florals to recall the finesse of a bygone time.

DISTILLERY:
Lady H Spirits, Auckland

BOTANICALS:
Juniper, Coriander Seed, Cinnamon & Others

TASTING NOTES:
Cinnamon and coriander drive the nose, sweet nutty spice with delicate florals and coriander on the palate, light florals and coriander lingering to finish.

SERVING SUGGESTION:
Enjoy with Fever-Tree Aromatic Tonic Water.

Gin & Bare It Optical Illusion

40% ABV

A contemporary gin, Gin & Bare It Optical Illusion is a twist on their original gin named for the colour change from deep blue to purple that happens when it is mixed with tonic thanks to butterfly pea flower.

DISTILLERY:
Lammermoor Distillery, Lammermoor

BOTANICALS:
Juniper Butterfly Pea Flower & Others

TASTING NOTES:
Light coriander with a hint of caramel and earth on the nose, sweet upfront with light coriander and hints of florals on the palate, quick finish with a touch of coriander lasting.

SERVING SUGGESTION:
Enjoy with Fever-Tree Mediterranean Tonic Water.

Lavender Hill Lavender Infused Gin

40% ABV

A contemporary gin, Lavender Hill Lavender Infused Gin is made using the essential oils from their own commercial fields of 'Pacific Blue' English lavender (Angustifolia) which is hand harvested and extracted on their farm.

DISTILLERY:
Lavender Hill, Riverhead

BOTANICALS:
Juniper, Coriander Seed, Cassia, Angelica Root, Nutmeg, Citrus Peel, Tangerine, Orris Root, Star Anise, Anise, Lemon, Orange, Cardamom & Lavender

TASTING NOTES:
Soft and floral with hints of lavender on the nose, subtle sweetness from florals with spiced orange fruits and coriander on the palate, slightly nutty and dry finish.

SERVING SUGGESTION:
Enjoy with Fever-Tree Elderflower Tonic Water.

Lavender Hill Saffron Infused Gin
40% ABV

A contemporary Gin, Lavender Hill Saffron Infused Gin is made using 100% organic saffron from a partner farm in the South Island, producing a vibrant yellow colour.

DISTILLERY:
Lavender Hill, Riverhead

BOTANICALS:
Juniper, Coriander Seed, Cassia, Angelica Root, Nutmeg, Citrus Peel, Tangerine, Orris Root, Star Anise, Anise, Lemon, Orange, Cardamom & Saffron

TASTING NOTES:
Soft pine, coriander, and lemon on the nose, rush of saffron and coriander on the palate, sweet spice and citrus drive a soft finish.

SERVING SUGGESTION:
Enjoy with Fever-Tree Refreshingly Light Indian Tonic Water.

The Racketeer Spiced Gin
42% ABV

A contemporary gin, The Racketeer Spiced Gin is designed to fill you with the warming flavours of winter, including cinnamon, ginger, clove, and cardamom amongst its botanicals.

DISTILLERY:
Longshot Distillery, Rolleston

BOTANICALS:
Juniper, Almond, Cinnamon, Ginger, Clove, Cardamom, Allspice & Orange

TASTING NOTES:
Classic baking spice with warm orange on the nose, classic spice follows onto the palate with subtle sweetness from orange, warming spice with a hint of pepper to finish.

SERVING SUGGESTION:
Enjoy with Fever-Tree Aromatic Tonic Water.

The Racketeer Verbena Gin
42% ABV

A contemporary gin, The Racketeer Verbena Gin uses lemon verbena in place of traditional citrus, which contains citral (the main component in citrus peel oil), paired with elderberry and hawthorne.

DISTILLERY:
LongShot Distillery, Rolleston

BOTANICALS:
Juniper, Coriander Seed, Lemon Verbena, Elderberry, Hawthorne Berry & Cardamom

TASTING NOTES:
Herbal mint, steeped green tea and coriander on the nose, subtle verbena, coriander and sweet cardamom on the palate, coriander and cardamom warmth to finish.

SERVING SUGGESTION:
Enjoy with Fever-Tree Mediterranean Tonic Water.

Peninsula Gin
42% ABV

A contemporary gin, Peninsula Gin is their signature product, made to reflect traditional taste while acknowledging contemporary botanical influences.

DISTILLERY:
Lyttelton Distillery Company, Lyttelton

BOTANICALS:
Juniper, Manuka, Thyme, Citrus Peel, Geranium, Angelica Root, Cardamom, Coriander Seed & Grains of Paradise

TASTING NOTES:
Pronounced green herbs, cardamom and orange on the nose, upfront spice with subtle citrus and light grains of paradise on the palate, mentholic thyme and persistent cardamom to finish.

SERVING SUGGESTION:
Enjoy with Fever-Tree Premium Indian Tonic Water.

Mt. Fyffe Distillery Shearwater Gin
42% ABV

A contemporary gin, Mt. Fyffe Distillery Shearwater Gin takes inspiration from the Hutton's shearwater that nests in the local mountains and feeds in the sea by using seaweed from the local coast and blue borage from the mountains.

DISTILLERY:
Mt. Fyffe Distillery, Kaikoura

BOTANICALS:
Juniper, Coriander Seed, Angelica Root, Rosehip, Seaweed & Blue Borage

TASTING NOTES:
Borage flower and bold seaweed on the nose, slight floral sweetness with accented salinity and strong seaweed on the palate, sweet rosehip to finish.

SERVING SUGGESTION:
Enjoy with Fever-Tree Mediterranean Tonic Water.

Mt. Fyffe Distillery Woolshed Gin
42% ABV

A contemporary gin, Mt. Fyffe Distillery Woolshed Gin is named after the farm's woolshed near and around which many of the botanicals in its blend are found.

DISTILLERY:
Mt. Fyffe Distillery, Kaikoura

BOTANICALS:
Juniper, Coriander Seed, Angelica Root, Kanuka, Mint, Elderflower, Orris Root, Cassia, Nutmeg, Rosemary, Lime & Pink Peppercorn

TASTING NOTES:
Crushed mint with delicate pepper on the nose, mint and warm baking spice continue with pepper on the palate, spice heat mellows to finish.

SERVING SUGGESTION:
Enjoy with Fever-Tree Elderflower Tonic Water.

NDC Adorn Beauty Gin

42% ABV

A contemporary gin, NDC Adorn Beauty Gin is inspired by the botanicals found in luxury New Zealand skincare products including New Zealand flax seed, rose petals, organic rosehip, and chamomile.

DISTILLERY:
The National Distillery Co., Napier

BOTANICALS:
Juniper, Coriander Seed, Angelica Root, Cardamom, Orris Root, Cassia, Lemon Peel, Rosehip, Rose Petal, Chamomile, Flax Seed & Liquorice

TASTING NOTES:
Subtly sweet rose with chamomile flower on the nose, chamomile leads with bursting florals, cardamom and oily flax seed on the palate, musky orris to finish.

SERVING SUGGESTION:
Enjoy with Fever-Tree Elderflower Tonic Water.

NDC Hemp Gin
45% ABV

A contemporary gin, NDC Hemp Gin expands on their signature seven core gin aromatics by adding toasted hemp hearts and lashings of lemon peel.

DISTILLERY:
The National Distillery Co., Napier

BOTANICALS:
Juniper, Coriander Seed, Angelica Root, Manuka, Cardamom, Peppercorn, Almond, Liquorice, Hemp & Lemon Peel

TASTING NOTES:
Earthy herbs, fresh pepper and toasted spice on nose, cardamom with toasted spice and lifted lemon zest on the palate, dark earthy notes and pepper to finish.

SERVING SUGGESTION:
Enjoy with Fever-Tree Refreshingly Light Indian Tonic Water.

NDC Meow Lucky Gin
44% ABV

A contemporary gin, NDC Meow Lucky Gin was inspired by a love of Asian cuisine incorporating yuzu, Sichuan pepper, and gingko leaf into its botanical blend.

DISTILLERY:
The National Distillery Co., Napier

BOTANICALS:
Juniper, Coriander Seed, Angelica Root, Cassia, Orris Root, Cardamom, Yuzu Peel, Ginkgo Leaf & Sichuan Pepper

---

TASTING NOTES:
Cassia with fragrant mint and a touch of citrus on the nose, earthy spice with subtle yuzu and minty-pepper emphasize the palate, quick settling finish with hot tingling pepper.

SERVING SUGGESTION:
Enjoy with Fever-Tree Refreshingly Light Indian Tonic Water.

NDC New Zealand Native Gin
44% ABV

A contemporary gin, New Zealand Native Gin expands on their signature seven core gin aromatics by showcasing native kawakawa and karamu berries.

DISTILLERY:
The National Distillery Co., Napier

BOTANICALS:
Juniper, Coriander Seed, Angelica Root, Cardamom, Orris Root, Cassia, Lemon Peel, Hemp, Flax Seed, Kawakawa, Karamu & Liquorice

TASTING NOTES:
Earthy roots with supporting spice on the nose, kawakawa and liquorice lead with oily flax seed on the palate, hints of black tea and green forest floor to finish.

SERVING SUGGESTION:
Enjoy with Fever-Tree Mediterranean Tonic Water.

NDC Verdigris New Zealand Dry Gin

44% ABV

A contemporary gin, NDC Verdigris New Zealand Dry Gin is inspired by London Dry Gin and highlights native New Zealand flax seed among its botanicals.

DISTILLERY:
The National Distillery Co., Napier

BOTANICALS:
Juniper, Coriander Seed, Angelica Root, Cardamom, Orris Root, Cassia, Lemon Peel, Flax Seed & Liquorice

TASTING NOTES:
Tart citrus, vibrant coriander and cardamom on the nose, spice leads with earthy liquorice and oily flax seed on the palate, earthy, slightly nutty finish.

SERVING SUGGESTION:
Enjoy with Fever-Tree Mediterranean Tonic Water.

No8 Distillery Hibiscus Gin
42% ABV

A contemporary gin, No8 Distillery Hibiscus Gin is inspired by many years travelling, working, eating, and drinking in Asia and is imparted with a ruby red colour by the inclusion of hibiscus petals.

DISTILLERY:
No8 Distillery, Dunedin

BOTANICALS:
Juniper, Coriander Seed, Angelica Root, Orris Root, Hibiscus, Dried Bitter Orange Peel, Mandarin, Yuzu, Makrut Lime Leaf, Cardamom, Cinnamon, Ginger, Passionfruit & Gorse Flower

TASTING NOTES:
Bittersweet marmalade with hints of wild gorse on the nose, tea like astringency with soft herbs and citrus on the palate, hot spice with earthiness to finish.

SERVING SUGGESTION:
Enjoy with Fever-Tree Refreshingly Light Indian Tonic Water.

No8 Distillery Horopito Gin
42% ABV

A contemporary gin, No8 Distillery Horopito Gin is the result of many years of development using horopito foraged in the Silver Peaks northwest of Dunedin.

DISTILLERY:
No8 Distillery, Dunedin

BOTANICALS:
Juniper, Coriander Seed, Angelica Root, Orris Root, Orange, Cardamom, Cinnamon & Horopito Leaf

TASTING NOTES:
Piny juniper and soft spice on the nose, pronounced cardamom and cinnamon spice with horopito heat on the palate, baking spice lingers to finish.

SERVING SUGGESTION:
Enjoy with Fever-Tree Premium Indian Tonic Water.

Papaiti Gin Orchard

42% ABV

A contemporary gin, Papaiti Gin Orchard is their signature gin expression, made using a single-shot distillation of traditional and native botanicals infused with orchard pears from their property in Papaiti.

DISTILLERY:
Papaiti Gin, Upokongaro

BOTANICALS:
Juniper, Coriander Seed, Angelica Root, Liquorice, Cassia, Orris Root, Nutmeg, Lemon Peel, Lime Peel, Kawakawa Leaf & Pear

TASTING NOTES:
Herbal forward with warming nutmeg and cassia on the nose, initial kawakawa sweetness with cassia on the palate, mellowing spice and warming citrus depth to finish.

SERVING SUGGESTION:
Enjoy with Fever-Tree Mediterranean Tonic Water.

Premium
LIQUOR CO.

Sundown Original Dry Gin
40% ABV

A contemporary gin, Sundown Original Dry Gin is inspired by the natural beauty of New Zealand, blending traditional botanicals with natural kawakawa and horopito extracts, and water from the Tautau and Waiorohi streams.

DISTILLERY:
Premium Liquor Co., Auckland

BOTANICALS:
Juniper, Coriander Seed, Orris Root, Angelica Root, Citrus Peel, Kawakawa & Horopito

TASTING NOTES:
Bitter kawakawa tones lead the nose, strong herbal notes from kawakawa and sharp citrus peel on the palate, leading to a quick finish.

SERVING SUGGESTION:
Enjoy with Fever-Tree Mediterranean Tonic Water.

REEFTON DISTILLING CO.
WEST COAST—NEW ZEALAND
EST. 2017

Little Biddy Gin - Classic
40% ABV

A contemporary gin, Little Biddy Gin Classic makes use of several native botanicals including Toatoa, Tarata, Horopito, and Rimu, as well as the majestic Douglas Fir, which are all foraged locally prior to distillation.

DISTILLERY:
Reefton Distilling Co., Reefton

BOTANICALS:
Juniper, Horopito, Tarata, Toatoa, Rimu, Douglas Fir, Angelica Root, Cardamom, Cassia, Coriander Seed, Lemon Peel, Liquorice & Orris Root

TASTING NOTES:
Resinous pine, forest floor elements and a menthol character on the nose, pronounced forest notes with lemon peel and liquorice on the palate, bold forest notes continue to finish.

SERVING SUGGESTION:
Enjoy with Fever-Tree Aromatic Tonic Water.

PREMIUM SPIRITS

REEFTON
DISTILLING CO
WEST COAST—NEW ZEALAND
ESTᴅ 2017

Little Biddy Gin Snow
43% ABV

A contemporary Gin, Little Biddy Gin Snow is a limited edition that captures the fresh, native aromas of the West Coast rainforest's canopy after a rare snowfall, including freshly foraged snow and other botanicals chosen to give it a refreshing cooling effect.

DISTILLERY:
Reefton Distilling Co., Reefton

BOTANICALS:
Juniper, Angelica Root, Cardamom, Coriander Seed, Liquorice, Orris Root, Fresh Snow, Peppermint, Manuka, Lime, Lavender & Green Peppercorn

TASTING NOTES:
Forest floor elements with bold mint and lavender on the nose, damp forest leaves, resinous earthy bark and crushed mint on the palate, liquorice and persistent mint carry to finish.

SERVING SUGGESTION:
Enjoy with Fever-Tree Aromatic Tonic Water.

CRAFT DISTILLERS OF MARTINBOROUGH

Reid + Reid Zesty Lemon Gin
40% ABV

A contemporary gin, Reid + Reid Zesty Lemon Gin is designed to be a thirst quenching dry gin on a long hot day, after the classic combination of lemon and gin, and made using both vapour infusion and pot distillation techniques.

DISTILLERY:
Reid + Reid Distillery, Martinborough

BOTANICALS:
Juniper, Coriander Seed, Angelica Root, Manuka Leaf, Lemon Zest, Lemongrass, Lemon Verbena, Lemon Myrtle, Cardamom & Vanilla

TASTING NOTES:
Vibrant lemon, bitter Manuka and cardamom on the nose, savoury lemon with angelica and native earthy characters on the palate, warming lemongrass with angelica to finish.

SERVING SUGGESTION:
Enjoy with Fever-Tree Mediterranean Tonic Water.

ULTIMATE MIX
TOM COLLINS

Rifters Quartz Gin
42% ABV

A contemporary dry style gin, Rifters Quartz Gin is distilled in small batches and showcases the flavours of Central Otago, using locally foraged where possible, including wild thyme, MÐnuka, and Douglas fir.

DISTILLERY:
Arrowtown Distillery, Arrowtown

BOTANICALS:
Juniper, Coriander Seed, Angelica Root, Liquorice, Orris Root, Cardamom, Black Peppercorn, Elderberry, Douglas Fir Tip, Mint Tip, Wild Thyme, Manuka, Lemon Peel & Lime Peel

TASTING NOTES:
Minty freshness, pine resin and savoury herbs on the nose, subtle forest elements with wood spice and pepper on the palate, minty heat to finish.

SERVING SUGGESTION:
Enjoy with Fever-Tree Mediterranean Tonic Water.

NEW ZEALAND

NEW WORLD GIN

1743 Riot

42% ABV

A contemporary gin, Riot & Rose 1743 Riot is a modern take on the traditional London Dry style paying homage to the London Gin Riots of 1743 and the bold, herbaceous flavours of that era.

DISTILLERY:
Riot & Rose Spirits, Blenheim

BOTANICALS:
Juniper & Others

TASTING NOTES:
Liquorice and green herbaceous aromas on the nose, subtle spice and light juniper on the palate, light hints of citrus on the finish.

SERVING SUGGESTION:
Enjoy with Fever-Tree Mediterranean Tonic Water.

NEW ZEALAND

NEW WORLD GIN

1920 Rose
42% ABV

A contemporary gin, Riot & Rose 1920 Rose harks back to the romance and glamour of the Roaring Twenties, and the flavours that saw gin come into vogue during that era including rose petal and cinnamon.

DISTILLERY:
Riot & Rose Spirits, Blenheim

BOTANICALS:
Juniper, Rose Petal Cinnamon & Others

TASTING NOTES:
Manuka and juniper lead the nose, soft florals and cardamom spice on the palate, lasting liquorice root to finish.

SERVING SUGGESTION:
Enjoy with Fever-Tree Elderflower Tonic Water.

The Courage
42% ABV

A contemporary gin, Ruin Distillery The Courage is inspired by the connection of the term 'Dutch Courage' to soldiers through the makers' and Upper Hutt's pride in their own military histories.

DISTILLERY:
Ruin Distillery, Upper Hutt

BOTANICALS:
Juniper, Coriander Seed, Angelica Root, Liquorice, Wild Fennel Seed, Rosemary, Bay Leaf, Orris Root & Cassia

TASTING NOTES:
Characterful base provides fruity notes with hints of pepper on the nose, pronounced fennel and liquorice with rosemary on the palate, fennel and liquorice continue to finish.

SERVING SUGGESTION:
Enjoy with Fever-Tree Premium Indian Tonic Water.

The Valley
42% ABV

A contemporary gin, Ruin Distillery The Valley is made using their own grain neutral spirit fermented with champagne yeast, and infused with botanicals of which some are locally foraged.

DISTILLERY:
Ruin Distillery, Upper Hutt

BOTANICALS:
Juniper, Coriander Seed, Angelica Root, Liquorice, Wild Fennel Seed, Orange Zest, Lemon Zest, Black Peppercorn, Orris Root, Cassia & Kawakawa Leaf

TASTING NOTES:
Pronounced liquorice root with hints of kawakawa on the nose, bitter tea, oily spices and mentholic heat on the palate, hot pepper and fennel lead the finish.

SERVING SUGGESTION:
Enjoy with Fever-Tree Aromatic Tonic Water.

Chapter One

43% ABV

A contemporary gin, Sandymount Distillery Chapter One Gin is the first in their Chapter series which represents memory and connection to place, capturing the sandy stretches of Penguin Beach, the scent of bright yellow lupins, and warmth of the summer sun.

DISTILLERY:
Sandymount Distillery, Otago Peninsula

BOTANICALS:
Juniper, Coriander Seed, Fennel Seed, Cardamom, Angelica Root, Orris Root, Cinnamon, Lemon & Orange

TASTING NOTES:
Cardamom and fennel shine on the nose, cardamom and fennel continue with a touch of orange on the palate, warming spice with citrus to finish.

SERVING SUGGESTION:
Enjoy with Fever-Tree Aromatic Tonic Water.

Chapter Two
44% ABV

A contemporary gin, Sandymount Distillery Chapter Two is the second in their Chapter series which represents memory and connection to place, capturing the taste of passionfruit, the smell of vines, damp grass, and the shade of the bush canopy from carefree and adventurous teenage years.

DISTILLERY:
Sandymount Distillery, Otago Peninsula

BOTANICALS:
Juniper, Coriander Seed, Rock Melon, Mango, Ti Kouka Bark, Cardamom, Angelica Root, Orris Root, Cinnamon, Lemon & Orange

TASTING NOTES:
Bright citrus, distinct rock melon and a touch of spice on the nose, pronounced coriander, angelica and cardamom on the palate, earthy spice and lemon to finish.

SERVING SUGGESTION:
Enjoy with Fever-Tree Mediterranean Tonic Water.

Tī Kōuka Forest Gin
42% ABV

Sandymount Distillery Ti Kouka Forest Gin showcases vibrant and versatile native New Zealand botanicals, taking inspiration from the Ti Kouka tree which is their distillery's symbol.

DISTILLERY:
Sandymount Distillery, Otago Peninsula

BOTANICALS:
Juniper, Coriander Seed, Cardamom, Harakeke, Horopito, Tarata, Manuka, Ti Kouka Bark, Kawakawa, Angelica Root, Orris Root, Cinnamon, Lemon & Orange

TASTING NOTES:
Forest floor woods with strong cardamom on the nose, initial resin with a touch of horopito and strong cardamom on the palate, light orange peel with persistent spice to finish.

SERVING SUGGESTION:
Enjoy with Fever-Tree Premium Indian Tonic Water.

SCAPEGRACE™
NEW ZEALAND DISTILLING CO

Scapegrace Black
41.6% ABV

A contemporary gin, Scapegrace Black Gin is the world's first black gin. Achieved through the use of aronia berry, saffron, pineapple, butterfly pea flower, and sweet potato. When paired with tonic its colour changes from black to purple.

DISTILLERY:
Scapegrace Distilling Co., Bendigo

BOTANICALS:
Juniper, Aronia Berry, Sweet Potato, Butterfly Pea Flower, Saffron, Pineapple & Others

TASTING NOTES:
Fresh pineapple, tart berry and subtle juniper on the nose, berry sweetness with pineapple and developing savoury characters on the palate, sweet thickness to finish.

SERVING SUGGESTION:
Enjoy with Fever-Tree Mediterranean Tonic Water.

STORM
STORMONLINE.COM

STORM Black Wolf Gin
44% ABV

A contemporary gin, STORM Black Wolf Gin is a collaboration between Storm clothing and The National Distillery Company made with lashings of lemon and lime peel.

DISTILLERY:
The National Distillery Co., Napier

BOTANICALS:
Juniper, Lemon, Lime, Orris Root, Angelica Root & Others

TASTING NOTES:
Earthy forest floor with coriander and hints of lemon zest on the nose, black pepper, lemon and earthy roots on the palate, clean quick finish.

SERVING SUGGESTION:
Enjoy with Fever-Tree Premium Indian Tonic Water.

Strange Nature Gin

44% ABV

A contemporary gin, Strange Nature Gin is a grape-based gin made using alcohol extracted from Sauvignon Blanc wine using spinning cone technology that preserves aromas and flavours.

DISTILLERY:
The Spirits Workshop Distillery, Christchurch

BOTANICALS:
Juniper

TASTING NOTES:
Stone fruit, passionfruit, lime and damp cut grass on the nose, caramelised apricots, tart lime and passionfruit accented by juniper on the palate, long fruity citrus driven finish.

SERVING SUGGESTION:
Enjoy with Fever-Tree Refreshingly Light Indian Tonic Water.

Victor Gin Lime Leaf
42% ABV

A contemporary gin, Victor Gin Lime Leaf expands on their Heavy Botanical gin's core flavours and concept with the single addition of makrut lime in its botanicals.

DISTILLERY:
Thomson Whisky Distillery, Riverhead

BOTANICALS:
Juniper, Lemon, Lemongrass, Cardamom, Coriander Seed & Makrut Lime

TASTING NOTES:
Bright lemongrass, lime leaf and soft green herbs on the nose, citrus peel and rounded warm spices on the palate, peppery spice and sweet citrus to finish.

SERVING SUGGESTION:
Enjoy with Fever-Tree Mediterranean Tonic Water.

Waiheke Distilling Co. Spirit of Waiheke

42% ABV

A contemporary gin, Waiheke Distilling Co. Spirit of Waiheke is designed to pay homage to its island provenance, embodying the land, wind, and sea around Waiheke.

DISTILLERY:
Waiheke Distilling Co.,
Waiheke Island

BOTANICALS:
Juniper & Others

TASTING NOTES:
Lifted citrus and green bush herbs on the nose, minerality leads with lemon and vegetal quality on the palate, astringent with hints of olive leaf on the finish.

SERVING SUGGESTION:
Enjoy with Fever-Tree Mediterranean Tonic Water.

Wild Diamond Black Gin
42% ABV

A contemporary gin, Wild Diamond Black Gin uses their Rare Dry Gin as a base infused with additional botanicals including Dutch cocoa, imparting an inky black colour.

DISTILLERY:
Wild Diamond Distillery, Queenstown

BOTANICALS:
Juniper, Coriander Seed, Angelica Root, Cassia, Liquorice Extract, Orris Root, Cardamom, Chamomile, Lavender, Hypericum, Rosehip, Astragalus, Elderflower, Cocoa & Others

TASTING NOTES:
Strong cacao nib with vanilla cake batter on the nose, cocoa and vanilla cake continue with light hints of coffee on the palate, mellowing dark notes to finish.

SERVING SUGGESTION:
Enjoy with Fever-Tree Ginger Ale.

WILD DIAMOND

Wild Diamond Rare Dry Gin

42% ABV

A contemporary gin, Wild Diamond Rare Dry Gin is a limited edition premium batch with botanicals including rosehip, elderflower, lavender, and astragalus.

DISTILLERY:
Wild Diamond Distillery, Queenstown

BOTANICALS:
Juniper, Coriander Seed, Angelica Root, Cassia, Liquorice Extract, Cinnamon, Almond, Manuka, Rosehip, Elderflower, Lavender, Astragalus & Others

TASTING NOTES:
Floral elderflower, almond, and rosehip on the nose, bright citrus, piny juniper and light florals on the palate, bitter herbs lead a mellowing finish.

SERVING SUGGESTION:
Enjoy with Fever-Tree Elderflower Tonic Water.

NAVY STRENGTH

NAVY STRENGTH GIN

Gins bottled at 54.5% ABV (alcohol by volume) and above.

———————

Broken Heart Navy Strength Gin
57% ABV

A navy gin with a potency of 57%, Broken Heart Navy Strength Gin is based on capturing the essence of their original Gin but with a stronger botanical flavour and impact.

DISTILLERY:
Broken Heart Spirits, Arrow Junction

BOTANICALS:
Juniper, Coriander Seed, Lavender, Angelica Root, Citrus, Orange Flower, Hops, Ginger, Pimento & Cinnamon

TASTING NOTES:
Green herbs with soft pine on the nose, bitter herbs with strong citrus and supporting juniper on the palate, clean lingering herbs and citrus to finish.

SERVING SUGGESTION:
Enjoy with Fever-Tree Mediterranean Tonic Water.

DANCING SANDS DISTILLERY

Dancing Sands Wasabi Gin
58% ABV

A navy gin with a potency of 58%, Dancing Sands Wasabi Gin is made using locally grown wasabi, available thanks to conditions found in the river downstream from Te Waikoropupu Springs, following 12 months of recipe development.

DISTILLERY:
Dancing Sands Distillery, Takaka

BOTANICALS:
Juniper, Coriander Seed, Almond, Liquorice, Angelica Root, Wasabi, Kelp, Orange & Horopito

TASTING NOTES:
Coriander and angelica with subtle horopito on the nose, light juniper, coriander and hints of horopito on the palate, morphs into an intense wasabi heat with persistent coriander to finish.

SERVING SUGGESTION:
Enjoy with Fever-Tree Premium Indian Tonic Water.

HERRICK CREEK

Nine Fathoms Canterbury Gin

57% ABV

A navy gin with a potency of 57%, Herrick Creek Nine Fathoms Canterbury Gin is named for and made in the spirit of a small passage between the mainland and Cooper Island in Fiordland, where moose are said to have been spotted.

2021 TASTERS' PICK — Guide to New Zealand Gin

DISTILLERY:
Herrick Creek Distillery, Christchurch

BOTANICALS:
Juniper, Coriander Seed, Angelica Root, Hop, Orange, Lemon, Cucumber, Horopito & Kiwifruit

TASTING NOTES:
Complex fruits, lifted citrus and bold pepper on the nose, citrus, bitter hop, and tart fruit lead the palate, horopito heat with hints of coriander and juniper to finish.

SERVING SUGGESTION:
Enjoy with Fever-Tree Premium Indian Tonic Water.

Island Gin Navy Strength
57% ABV

A navy strength gin with a potency of 57%, Island Gin Navy Strength uses both Manuka and bush honey from Great Barrier Island and is nicknamed 'Shark Alley' because it is "not for the faint hearted".

DISTILLERY:
Island Gin Distillery, Great Barrier

BOTANICALS:
Manuka Honey, Bush Honey, Coriander Seed, Lemon Myrtle & Others

TASTING NOTES:
Herbaceous elements with earthy coriander and light juniper on the nose, strong pepper with green leaf herbs and striking lemon myrtle on the palate, heated spice to finish.

SERVING SUGGESTION:
Enjoy with Fever-Tree Mediterranean Tonic Water.

Lighthouse Gin Hawthorn Edition
57% ABV

A navy gin with a potency of 57%, Lighthouse Gin Hawthorn Edition is inspired by a Wellington institution, the Hawthorn Lounge, which is an intimate speakeasy that focuses on cocktails.

VOL. 3 — HIGHLY COMMENDED

ULTIMATE MIX — NEGRONI

2021 — TASTERS' PICK

DISTILLERY:
Lighthouse Gin Distillery, Martinborough

BOTANICALS:
Juniper, Coriander Seed, Yen Ben Lemon Zest, Navel Orange Zest, Cinnamon, Almond, Cassia, Orris Root & Liquorice

TASTING NOTES:
Classic juniper, coriander and earthy roots on the nose, slightly creamy lemon with coriander and root spice on the palate, lingering baking spice to finish.

SERVING SUGGESTION:
Enjoy with Fever-Tree Aromatic Tonic Water.

NDC Old Navy - Navy Strength Gin

58% ABV

A navy gin with a potency of 58%, NDC New Zealand Navy Strength Gin is inspired by a classic London Dry Gin with a tip of the hat to the pirates of old.

DISTILLERY:
The National Distillery Co., Napier

BOTANICALS:
Juniper, Lemon Peel, Native Flax Seed & Others

TASTING NOTES:
Hot peppery heat with bitter lemon on the nose, soft spice, light citrus and oily flax seed with emphasised heat on the palate, astringent menthol led finish.

SERVING SUGGESTION:
Enjoy with Fever-Tree Premium Indian Tonic Water.

Roots Norwester Navy Strength Dry Gin

54.5% ABV

A navy gin with a potency of 54.5%, Roots Norwester Navy Strength Dry Gin is a stronger bottling of their Marlborough Dry Gin with the addition of giant kelp from Akaroa and hemp seed from the Hawke's Bay.

GUIDE TO NEW ZEALAND GIN — VOL. 3 — HIGHLY COMMENDED

DISTILLERY:
Elemental Distillers, Marlborough

BOTANICALS:
Juniper, Coriander Seed, Grapefruit, Hop, Kawakawa Berries, Gorse Flowers, Hemp Seed & Giant Kelp

TASTING NOTES:
Grassy notes with funky hops, native herbs and citrus on the nose, kawakawa pepper, bittersweet grapefruit and supporting juniper on the palate, grapefruit peel lingers to finish.

SERVING SUGGESTION:
Enjoy with Fever-Tree Mediterranean Tonic Water.

SCAPEGRACE
NEW ZEALAND DISTILLING CO

Scapegrace Gold
57% ABV

A navy gin with a potency of 57%, Scapegrace Dry Gin Gold is a London Dry Gin with three layers of citrus: orange, lemon, and tangerine, which won the IWSC trophy for World's Best London Dry in 2018.

DISTILLERY:
Scapegrace Distilling Co.,
Bendigo

BOTANICALS:
Juniper, Lemon Peel, Orange Peel, Coriander Seed, Cardamom, Nutmeg, Angelica Root, Liquorice, Orris Root, Clove, Cinnamon, Cassia & Tangerine

TASTING NOTES:
Fragrant lemon, juniper and classic baking spice on the nose, slightly sweet citrus with supporting spice on the palate, hints of coriander and clove on the finish.

SERVING SUGGESTION:
Enjoy with Fever-Tree Premium Indian Tonic Water.

The Vicar's Son The Holy Spirit Navy Strength

57% ABV

A navy gin with a potency of 57%, The Vicar's Son Gin The Holy Spirit Navy Strength was made with the goal of allowing the saffron in their The Holy Spirit gin to shine more at a higher ABV.

DISTILLERY:
The Vicar's Son, Auckland

BOTANICALS:
Juniper, Saffron, Pink Peppercorn, Rosemary Flower, Angelica Root, Cassia, Liquorice, Poppy Seed, Cardamom, Nutmeg, Dried Lemonade Lemon Zest & Others

TASTING NOTES:
Zesty lemonade with light florals and a touch of grain on the nose, light juniper and lemonade continuing with delicate green pepper on the palate, coriander and peppercorn mellow to finish.

SERVING SUGGESTION:
Enjoy with Fever-Tree Premium Indian Tonic Water.

PINK

Distilled gins that have natural Pink colouring due to the redistillation of berries, red fruits or pink botanicals.

1919 Pink Gin
41% ABV

A pink gin, 1919 Pink Gin is inspired by gin and bitters, and distilled using raspberries and Auckland grown strawberries which capture the taste of summer and impart a pale pink colour.

GUIDE TO NEW ZEALAND GIN — VOL. 3 — TASTERS' PICK

GUIDE TO NEW ZEALAND GIN — 2021 — TASTERS' PICK

GUIDE TO NEW ZEALAND GIN — 2020 — TASTERS' PICK

DISTILLERY:
1919 Distilling, Auckland

BOTANICALS:
Juniper, Coriander Seed, Green Cardamom, Lemon Peel, Orange Peel, Angelica Root, Cherries, Manuka Honey, Cinnamon, Strawberry & Raspberry

TASTING NOTES:
Delicate red berries with supporting dry spice on the nose, tart cherry, cardamom and coriander lead with soft juniper on the palate, lingering red fruits and mellowing spice to finish.

SERVING SUGGESTION:
Enjoy with Fever-Tree Aromatic Tonic Water.

batch10 Pink Gin
40% ABV

A pink gin, batch10 Pink honours the historic recipe by balancing the light spice of bitters with the freshness of pomegranate in combination with their smooth classic gin, giving it a vibrant pink colour.

DISTILLERY:
batch10 Spirits, Puhoi

BOTANICALS:
Juniper, Coriander Seed, Cassia, Angelica Root, Nutmeg, Citrus Peel, Tangerine, Orris Root, Star Anise, Anise, Lemon, Orange, Cardamom, Pomegranate & Bitters

TASTING NOTES:
Subtle spice and fruit notes on the nose, syrupy pomegranate, anise and nutmeg on the palate, soft mellowing spice drives the finish.

SERVING SUGGESTION:
Enjoy with Fever-Tree Aromatic Tonic Water.

JUNO GIN

Juno Spring 2022
44% ABV

A pink gin, Juno Spring 2022 is inspired by the first picnics of the year, fresh green grass, and strolls through the blossoms, with a light pink hue and featuring artwork by Jade Turner on the bottle.

DISTILLERY:
Begin Distilling, New Plymouth

BOTANICALS:
Juniper, Coriander Seed, Angelica Root, Orris Root, Lemon, Raspberry, Mint, Black Peppercorn, Cassia, Makrut Lime & Cardamom

TASTING NOTES:
Funky mint and earthy roots lead the nose, candied red fruit upfront with strong earthy cassia and warming pepper on the palate, heat develops with lasting earthy spice to finish.

SERVING SUGGESTION:
Enjoy with Fever-Tree Premium Lemonade.

Laughing Club Gin 1928 Pink
44% ABV

A pink Gin, Laughing Club Gin 1928 Pink uses their original gin as its base with the addition of boysenberry, beetroot, gentian, and caramel, with a rosy pink colour.

DISTILLERY:
Kiwi Spirit Distillery, Motupipi

BOTANICALS:
Juniper, Coriander Seed, Peppercorn, Cubeb, Lemon, Orris Root, Liquorice, Boysenberry, Beetroot, Gentian & Caramel

TASTING NOTES:
Light cream with a touch of strawberry and juniper on the nose, moderate sweetness with light berry tones and a touch of peppery heat on the palate, leads to a quick finish.

SERVING SUGGESTION:
Enjoy with Fever-Tree Wild Raspberry Tonic Water.

Pink & White Geothermal Gin Pink

45% ABV

A pink gin, Pink & White Geothermal Gin Pink combines blueberries, strawberries, and raspberries amongst other botanicals, which impart it with a pale pink colour.

DISTILLERY:
Pink & White - Geothermal Gin, Rotorua

BOTANICALS:
Juniper, Raspberry, Blueberry, Strawberry, Clove & Others

TASTING NOTES:
Pithy raspberry jam and floral earth on the nose, pithy raspberry continues with supporting earthy characters on the palate, red fruits with perfume like notes and a touch of pepper to finish.

SERVING SUGGESTION:
Enjoy with Fever-Tree Wild Raspberry Tonic Water.

Little Biddy Gin - Pink

43% ABV

A pink gin, Little Biddy Gin Pink has been crafted to utilise the natural colour, sweetness, and depth of local New Zealand cherries, with a rich purple-pink colour.

DISTILLERY:
Reefton Distilling Co., Reefton

BOTANICALS:
Juniper, Cherry, Lemon, Orange, Pink Peppercorn, Green Peppercorn, Angelica Root, Nutmeg, Cardamom, Cassia, Coriander Seed, Liquorice & Orris Root

TASTING NOTES:
Spice forward with dominant cassia and nutmeg on the nose, cassia continues strongly with bitter red fruit notes on the palate, spice fades quickly to finish.

SERVING SUGGESTION:
Enjoy with Fever-Tree Aromatic Tonic Water.

FLAVOURED

FLAVOURED GIN

Gins with additional flavour influence, often from fruits or flavourings post distillation through a variety of methods.

GIN LIQUEUR

Gins with the addition of sugar, sweetened over a certain volume post distillation.

SLOE GIN

Distilled gins steeped in sloe berries and mixed with sugar post distillation.

1919 Pineapple Bits Gin
41% ABV

A flavoured gin, 1919 Pineapple Bits Gin is a limited release in their Kiwiana Collection paying homage to a classic Kiwi lolly tasting of pineapple and chocolate, with a pale yellow colour.

DISTILLERY:
1919 Distilling, Auckland

BOTANICALS:
Juniper, Coriander Seed, Lemon Peel, Orange Peel, Angelica Root, Pineapple & Cacao Nib

TASTING NOTES:
Pineapple, lemon, and cocoa on the nose, pineapple and cocoa lead with a touch of juniper and coriander on the palate, root spice and mellowing citrus on the finish.

SERVING SUGGESTION:
Enjoy with Fever-Tree Refreshingly Light Indian Tonic Water.

Hector's French Farm Petit Pinot Gin

42% ABV

A flavoured gin, Hector's French Farm Petit Pinot Gin is named for the Hector's dolphins that swim off of Akaroa and takes its flavour profile from botanicals foraged around Banks Peninsula, along with French Peak Vineyard Pinot Noir, Syrah, and classic botanicals, which gives it ruby red colour.

DISTILLERY:
Akaroa Craft Distillery, Akaroa

BOTANICALS:
Juniper, French Peak Pinot Noir, Syrah, Kelp, Thyme, Lemon Myrtle, Orange, Lavender, Cardamom, Cinnamon, Angelica Root, Orris Root, Liquorice & Coriander Seed

TASTING NOTES:
Rich red fruit with an acidic pulpy wine character on the nose, initial juniper with strong thyme and lemon myrtle on the palate, floral lavender and sweet lemon myrtle to finish.

SERVING SUGGESTION:
Enjoy with Fever-Tree Premium Indian Tonic Water.

Blush Boysenberry Gin
37.5% ABV

A flavoured Gin, Blush Boysenberry Gin is the world's first boysenberry gin, sourcing its star ingredient fresh from Nelson which imparts a bold, dark red colour.

DISTILLERY:
Blush Gin Ltd., Auckland

BOTANICALS:
Juniper, Boysenberry, Citrus Peel, Anise, Cardamom & Angelica Root

TASTING NOTES:
Sweet boysenberry and anise on the nose, pronounced berry sweetness with light supporting spice on the palate, red fruit notes lead a sweet finish.

SERVING SUGGESTION:
Enjoy with Fever-Tree Wild Raspberry Tonic Water.

Blush Rhubarb Gin

37.5% ABV

A flavoured gin, the very first batch of Blush Rhubarb Gin was actually made in a 500ml jam jar and has a deep pink colour.

DISTILLERY:
Blush Gin Ltd., Auckland

BOTANICALS:
Juniper, Rhubarb, Liquorice, Coriander Seed, Cassia, Angelica Root, Nutmeg, Citrus Peel, Tangerine, Orris Root & Star Anise

TASTING NOTES:
Rhubarb and root spice lead the nose, sweet fruity rhubarb with light supporting spice on the palate, fruity sweetness leads the finish.

SERVING SUGGESTION:
Enjoy with Fever-Tree Elderflower Tonic Water.

Blush Summer Citrus Gin

41.08% ABV

A flavoured gin, Blush Summer Citrus Gin is infused with citrus from sunny Kerikeri and rhubarb, which give it a cloudy pale pink colour.

DISTILLERY:
Blush Gin Ltd., Auckland

BOTANICALS:
Juniper, Rhubarb, Liquorice, Coriander Seed, Cassia, Angelica Root, Nutmeg, Citrus Peel, Navel Orange, Lemon, Tangerine, Orris Root & Star Anise

TASTING NOTES:
Candied lemons and orange on the nose, astringent marmalade character of lemon and orange on the palate, continuing oily citrus leads a hot finish.

SERVING SUGGESTION:
Enjoy with Fever-Tree Blood Orange Soda.

BLUSH
TRIPLE DISTILLED | HANDCRAFTED | BATCH INFUSED

Weekender Lemon Gin
41% ABV

A flavoured gin, Weekender Lemon Gin is a take on the proverbial phrase "When life gives you lemons", but making a zesty gin instead of lemonade.

DISTILLERY:
Blush Gin Ltd., Auckland

BOTANICALS:
Juniper, Coriander Seed, Angelica Root, Orange Peel, Lemon Peel, Orris Root & Lemon

TASTING NOTES:
Striking lemon peel on the nose, confectionary-like lemon peel sweetness with a tingle of pepper on the palate, candied lemon peel to finish.

SERVING SUGGESTION:
Enjoy with Fever-Tree Refreshingly Light Indian Tonic Water.

BLUSH
TRIPLE DISTILLED | HANDCRAFTED | BATCH INFUSED

Weekender Orange Gin
41% ABV

A flavoured gin,, Weekender Orange Gin showcases sweet navel oranges along with lemon peel against its juniper and spice.

DISTILLERY:
Blush Gin Ltd., Auckland

BOTANICALS:
Juniper, Coriander Seed, Angelica Root, Orange Peel, Lemon Peel, Orris Root & Navel Orange

TASTING NOTES:
Bright orange peel with a hint of blossom on the nose, fresh slightly bitter orange peel with pepper heat on the palate, pithy orange and pepper to finish.

SERVING SUGGESTION:
Enjoy with Fever-Tree Refreshingly Light Indian Tonic Water.

BLUSH
TRIPLE DISTILLED | HANDCRAFTED | BATCH INFUSED

Weekender Peach Gin
41% ABV

A flavoured gin,, Weekender Peach Gin is the only New Zealand made peach gin, packed full of flavour and sweetness from its use of ripe juicy peaches.

DISTILLERY:
Blush Gin Ltd., Auckland

BOTANICALS:
Juniper, Coriander Seed, Angelica Root, Orange Peel, Lemon Peel, Orris Root & Peach

TASTING NOTES:
Richly-sweet peach with a hint of florals on the nose, floral peach drives and dominates the palate, confectionary peaches and cream lolly like note to finish.

SERVING SUGGESTION:
Enjoy with Fever-Tree Refreshingly Light Indian Tonic Water.

BROKEN HEART
— GIN —
Distilled in the Pure South of New Zealand

Broken Heart Angel's Share Collectors Edition

40% ABV

A flavoured gin, Broken Heart Angel's Share Collectors Edition is a special edition made in small batches and inspired by their original gin, playing on the frontiers of balance, with an oaky gold colour.

DISTILLERY:
Broken Heart Spirits, Arrow Junction

BOTANICALS:
Juniper, Coriander Seed, Citrus, Angelica Root, Lavender, Orange Flower, Hop, Ginger, Pimento, Cinnamon & Basil

TASTING NOTES:
Steeped basil with fragrant ginger on the nose, soaked basil with coriander and supporting baking spice on the palate, aniseed tinge with ginger heat to finish.

SERVING SUGGESTION:
Enjoy with Fever-Tree Mediterranean Tonic Water.

BROKEN HEART
GIN
Distilled in the Pure South of New Zealand

Bella Wild Plum Gin Elixir

25% ABV

A gin liqueur, Bella Wild Plum Gin Elixir is made using juice from wild plums picked in Dublin Bay by well-known New Zealand Chef, Annabel Langbein and her family, and blended with 18 different aromatics to be a liqueur for all occasions.

DISTILLERY:
Broken Heart Spirits, Arrow Junction

BOTANICALS:
Juniper, Coriander Seed, Seville Orange, Plum, Vanilla, Star Anise & Others

TASTING NOTES:
Creamy almond, juicy crushed plum, baking spice and juniper on the nose, stewed plums with coriander, orange and pronounced star anise on the palate, warming spice with deep-dark tannic fruit to finish.

SERVING SUGGESTION:
Enjoy Neat or with Fever-Tree Premium Lemonade.

GUIDE TO NEW ZEALAND GIN — VOL. 3 — HIGHLY COMMENDED

Broken Heart Pinot Noir Gin

40% ABV

A flavoured gin, Broken Heart Pinot Noir Gin uses their original dry Gin as its base which is cold-soaked in Central Otago pinot noir grapes, creating a soft and sweet spirit with an autumn red colour.

DISTILLERY:
Broken Heart Spirits, Arrow Junction

BOTANICALS:
Juniper, Coriander Seed, Lavender, Angelica Root, Citrus, Orange Flower, Hops, Ginger, Pimento, Cinnamon & Pinot Noir Grapes

TASTING NOTES:
Fruity sultana, fig, and crisp buttery pastry on the nose, sweet dried fruit dominates the palate, a dry and tannic finish.

SERVING SUGGESTION:
Enjoy with Fever-Tree Refreshingly Light Indian Tonic Water.

Broken Heart Quince Gin
40% ABV

A flavoured gin, Broken Heart Quince Gin uses their original dry Gin as its base which is cold-soaked in fresh organic quince, a fruit often symbolically associated with love, and has a rich amber colour.

DISTILLERY:
Broken Heart Spirits, Arrow Junction

BOTANICALS:
Juniper, Coriander Seed, Lavender, Angelica Root, Citrus, Orange Flower, Hops, Ginger, Pimento, Cinnamon & Quince

TASTING NOTES:
Tart quince and juniper lead the nose, tart quince continues with coriander and juniper supporting on the palate, developing herbaceous tones to finish.

SERVING SUGGESTION:
Enjoy with Fever-Tree Ginger Ale.

Broken Heart Rhubarb Gin

40% ABV

A flavoured gin, Broken Heart Rhubarb Gin uses their original dry Gin as its base which is infused with a combination of organic green, pink, and red rhubarb, resulting in a peachy pink colour.

DISTILLERY:
Broken Heart Spirits,
Arrow Junction

BOTANICALS:
Juniper, Coriander Seed, Lavender, Angelica Root, Citrus, Orange Flower, Hops, Ginger, Pimento, Cinnamon & Rhubarb

TASTING NOTES:
Earthy rhubarb and floral notes on the nose, soft baking spice, earthy roots and tart rhubarb on the palate, bitter juniper leads the finish.

SERVING SUGGESTION:
Enjoy with Fever-Tree Ginger Ale.

Black Doris Plum Gin
38% ABV

A flavoured Gin, Bureaucrats Black Doris Plum Wellington Gin includes a combination of Black Doris plums and spices, resulting in a delicate purple hue.

DISTILLERY:
Bureaucrats Gin Ltd., Wellington

BOTANICALS:
Juniper, Coriander Seed, Plum & Others

TASTING NOTES:
Earthy and delicate dry fruit on the nose, subtle spice with tart plum on the palate, coriander develops with a dry finish.

SERVING SUGGESTION:
Enjoy with Fever-Tree Aromatic Tonic Water.

Curiosity Gin - Pinot Barrel Sloe

27% ABV

A sloe gin, Curiosity Gin Pinot Barrel Sloe is made the traditional way by steeping sloe berries in their Curious Dry gin for several months using ex-Otago Pinot Noir barrels.

— VOL. 3 —
TASTERS' PICK
GUIDE TO NEW ZEALAND GIN

— 2021 —
HIGHLY COMMENDED
GUIDE TO NEW ZEALAND GIN

DISTILLERY:
The Spirits Workshop Distillery, Christchurch

BOTANICALS:
Juniper, Manuka Berry, Manuka Leaf, Coriander Seed, Cardamom, Orange Zest, Angelica Root, Lavender, Cinnamon & Star Anise (Steeped in Sloe Berries in ex-Pinot Noir Barrels)

TASTING NOTES:
Sloe berry and Pinot Noir tannins on the nose, sweet and smooth red fruit with soft baking spice and balanced sweetness on the palate, flavours continue to develop with mellowing spice to finish.

SERVING SUGGESTION:
Enjoy with Fever-Tree Refreshingly Light Indian Tonic Water.

Curiosity Gin - Ruby

37.5% ABV

A flavoured gin, Curiosity Gin Ruby is made by infusing their Curious Dry gin with fresh Otaki rhubarb stalks and a little added sweetness, resulting in a delicate red hue.

DISTILLERY:
The Spirits Workshop Distillery, Christchurch

BOTANICALS:
Juniper, Tarata, Kawakawa, Horopito, Manuka & Rhubarb

TASTING NOTES:
Candied-sweet rhubarb and earthy tarata on the nose, striking rhubarb sweetness with horopito pepper on the palate, thick sweet finish.

SERVING SUGGESTION:
Enjoy with Fever-Tree Refreshingly Light Indian Tonic Water.

Dancing Sands Sauvignon Blanc Gin

37.5% ABV

A flavoured gin, Dancing Sands Sauvignon Blanc Gin is made using a vacuum distillation process that infuses New Zealand sauvignon blanc wine with their Dry Gin while preserving the wine's original flavor.

DISTILLERY:
Dancing Sands Distillery, Takaka

BOTANICALS:
Juniper, Coriander Seed, Angelica Root, Manuka, Cardamom, Peppercorn, Almond & Liquorice (vacuum distilled with Sauvignon Blanc).

TASTING NOTES:
Astringent Sauvignon Blanc character with lime on the nose, fresh green grass with sweet and tangy citrus on the palate, green spice and pepper to finish.

SERVING SUGGESTION:
Enjoy with Fever-Tree Mediterranean Tonic Water.

Dancing Sands Sun-Kissed Gin

37.5% ABV

A flavoured gin, Dancing Sands Sun-Kissed Gin is made using fresh strawberries and locally sourced rhubarb, which are then candied before infusion, giving it a pale pink colour.

DISTILLERY:
Dancing Sands Distillery, Takaka

BOTANICALS:
Juniper, Coriander Seed, Angelica Root, Manuka, Cardamom, Peppercorn, Almond, Liquorice, Strawberry & Rhubarb

TASTING NOTES:
Sweet baking spice and red fruit on the nose, off-dry sweetness with green spice and pepper on the palate, lasting subtle red fruit sweetness to finish.

SERVING SUGGESTION:
Enjoy with Fever-Tree Wild Raspberry Tonic Water.

ELSEWHERE

TRIPLE GIN — HAND CRAFTED

Elsewhere Central Otago Triple Gin
42% ABV

A flavoured gin, Elsewhere Central Otago Triple Gin is a limited edition made using Bannockburn pinot noir grapes that are macerated in a triple gin for one year, giving it a rich red wine colour.

GUIDE TO NEW ZEALAND GIN — VOL. 3 — HIGHLY COMMENDED

DISTILLERY:
Elsewhere Gin, Christchurch

BOTANICALS:
Juniper, Coriander Seed, Angelica Root, Lemon, Kawakawa, Horopito, Pinot Noir, Red Cherry, Wild Thyme, Matagouri Blossom, Sweet Briar Rose & Otago Schist

TASTING NOTES:
Rich cherries, kawakawa and thyme lead the nose, strong cherry, minty-thyme and horopito spice developing on the palate, drying Chinese black tea note with persistent thyme to finish.

SERVING SUGGESTION:
Enjoy with Fever-Tree Mediterranean Tonic Water.

Forth Luck Chic Gin

40% ABV

A flavoured Gin, Forth Luck Chic Gin is their version of a pink gin, honouring their Premium Gin recipe by bringing together a balance of fruits and botanicals, with a ruby red colour.

DISTILLERY:
Forth Luck Distillery, Christchurch

BOTANICALS:
Juniper, Angelica Root, Liquorice, Coriander Seed, Orris Root, Hibiscus, Orange, Strawberry & Raspberry

---

TASTING NOTES:
Floral hibiscus and tart berry fruits on the nose, tart raspberry and light strawberry with coriander and angelica on the palate, light linger of hibiscus and raspberry seed to finish.

SERVING SUGGESTION:
Enjoy with Fever-Tree Wild Raspberry Tonic Water.

Good George Doris Plum Gin

40% ABV

A flavoured gin, Good George Doris Plum Gin is a spin on their original Day Off Gin, with an infusion of Doris plums and pink peppercorns, which impart a rich red colour.

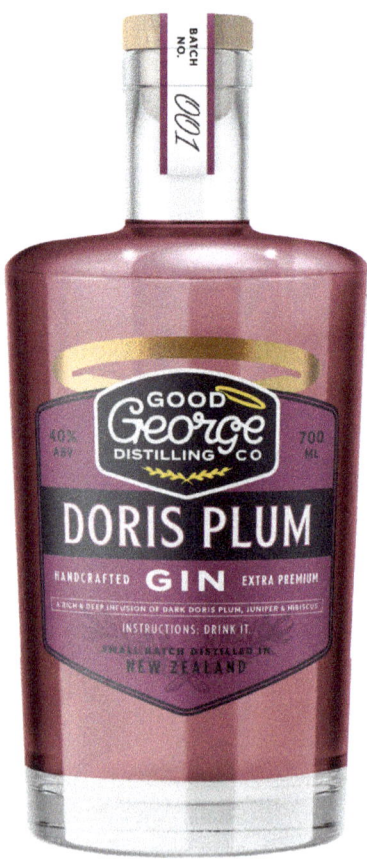

DISTILLERY:
Good George Distillery, Hamilton

BOTANICALS:
Juniper, Coriander Seed, Angelica Root, Liquorice, Pink Peppercorn, Rosehip, Cardamom, Star Anise, Bitter Orange Peel, Chamomile Flower, Black Doris Plum & Dried Hibiscus Flower

TASTING NOTES:
Sweet plum with hints of coriander and juniper on the nose, tart-juicy plum with supporting florals and orange on the palate, touches of rose and hibiscus drive a tea-like finish.

SERVING SUGGESTION:
Enjoy with Fever-Tree Premium Indian Tonic Water.

Posy Pink Gin Liqueur
38.5% ABV

A gin liqueur, Hastings Distillers Posy Pink Gin Liqueur combines the freshness of citrus and raspberries, which give it a delicate pink hue, with sweet and spicy notes.

DISTILLERY:
Hasting Distillers, Hastings

BOTANICALS:
Juniper, Lemon Peel, Allspice, Hibiscus, Raspberry, Cardamom, Lime, Lavender & Lemon Myrtle

TASTING NOTES:
Funky florals, pithy raspberry accented by cardamom and juniper on the nose, red fruits, green cardamom and juniper with a dry sweetness on the palate, lemon myrtle, fruity florals and warming spice to finish.

SERVING SUGGESTION:
Enjoy with Fever-Tree Refreshingly Light Indian Tonic Water.

Humdinger New Zealand Sloe Gin

27.7% ABV

A sloe gin, Humdinger New Zealand Sloe Gin is a limited release made by steeping Canterbury-grown sloe berries in one their gins, with a ruby red colour.

DISTILLERY:
Humdinger Distillery, Geraldine

BOTANICALS:
Juniper, Barley, Coriander Seed, Nutmeg, Liquorice, Angelica Root, Ginger, Lemon Peel, Orange Peel & Sloe Berry

TASTING NOTES:
Red currant, soft baking spice and marzipan on the nose, bright currant notes with strong almond accompanied by baking spice on the palate, lingering red currant with mellowing baking spice to finish.

SERVING SUGGESTION:
Enjoy with Fever-Tree Premium Indian Tonic Water.

Damson Plum & Blackberry Gin Liqueur
32% ABV

A gin liqueur, imagination Damson Plum & Blackberry New Zealand Gin Liqueur is inspired by an old English recipe that highlights New Zealand's seasonal autumn produce, including plums that were macerated in their Dry Gin for four months, giving it a deep purple red colour.

DISTILLERY:
imagination, Reikorangi

BOTANICALS:
Juniper, Coriander Seed, Cinnamon, Liquorice, Orris Root, Orange, Lime, Lemon, Manuka, Damson Plum & Blackberry

TASTING NOTES:
Soft baking spice with cinnamon, orris root and liquorice on the nose, tart-juicy plum with fruity berry notes on the palate, oily citrus peel to finish.

SERVING SUGGESTION:
Enjoy with Fever-Tree Lemonade.

Lewis Farms Strawberry Gin

40% ABV

A flavoured gin, imagination Lewis Farms Strawberry Gin is an ode to Christmas and the Kiwi summer, with a punnet of strawberries in every litre from the Lewis family farm in Levin, imparting a rich strawberry jam colour.

DISTILLERY:
imagination, Reikorangi

BOTANICALS:
Juniper, Coriander Seed, Manuka, Liquorice, Cinnamon, Lemon, Lime, Orange & Strawberries

TASTING NOTES:
Stewed strawberry jam and creamy vanilla on the nose, a hint of juniper with off-dry creamy strawberry and tart green herbs on the palate, slightly bitter red fruit note to finish.

SERVING SUGGESTION:
Enjoy with Fever-Tree Lemonade.

Reikorangi Rhubarb & Raspberry Gin
38% ABV

A flavoured Gin, imagination Reikorangi Rhubarb & Raspberry New Zealand Gin is inspired by the New Zealand summer, using raspberries macerated in a floral dry gin and blended with slowly extracted rhubarb juice, which gives it a bold pink-red colour.

DISTILLERY:
imagination, Reikorangi

BOTANICALS:
Juniper, Coriander Seed, Angelica Root, Manuka, Cardamom, Peppercorn, Almond & Liquorice

TASTING NOTES:
Raspberry, vanilla and rhubarb on the nose, warming baking spice, liquorice and tart fruitiness on the palate, subtle spice leads a very dry finish.

SERVING SUGGESTION:
Enjoy with Fever-Tree Wild Raspberry Tonic Water.

Juniper Jinn Liqueur
27.5% ABV

A gin liqueur, Juniper Distillery Juniper Jinn Liqueur is made with lemon and lavender, along with ube which gives it a rich purple colour, then sealed with purple wax.

DISTILLERY:
Juniper Distillery, Rangiora

BOTANICALS:
Juniper, Lavender, Lemon & Ube

TASTING NOTES:
Hints of rose water and a funky base character on the nose, sweetness drives with striking florals on the palate, leading to a quick finish.

SERVING SUGGESTION:
Enjoy with Fever-Tree Elderflower Tonic Water.

Rose Jinn Liqueur

27.5% ABV

A gin liqueur, Juniper Distillery Rose Jinn Liqueur is made with rose water and rose syrup which give it a Turkish delight flavour and candy pink colour, sealed with pink wax.

DISTILLERY:
Juniper Distillery, Rangiora

BOTANICALS:
Juniper, Lavender, Citrus, Rose Water & Rose Syrup

TASTING NOTES:
Rose water, Turkish delight, and characterful base notes lead the nose, light rose water drives Turkish delight-like flavour on the palate, leading to a quick finish.

SERVING SUGGESTION:
Enjoy with Fever-Tree Elderflower Tonic Water.

Trader Jinn Liqueur

27.5% ABV

A gin liqueur, Juniper Distillery Trader Jinn Liqueur evokes a Christmas Pudding with the blend of spices among its botanicals and sweetness, sealed with green wax.

DISTILLERY:
Juniper Distillery, Rangiora

BOTANICALS:
Juniper, Lavender, Citrus, Star Anise, Cinnamon, Clove, Cardamom & Others

TASTING NOTES:
Nutty spice with characterful base notes on the nose, sugar thickness with hints of light baking spice on the palate, rich sugariness to finish.

SERVING SUGGESTION:
Enjoy with Fever-Tree Premium Indian Tonic Water.

Eliza's Claim Ruby Gin

47% ABV

A flavoured Gin, Eliza's Claim Ruby Gin is named in memory of a pioneering goldmine in the Kaimai Ranges and made using 12 botanicals then infused with hibiscus, which gives it a ruby red colour.

DISTILLERY:
Kaimai Brewing & Distilling Co., Waikino

BOTANICALS:
Juniper, Angelica Root, Hibiscus, Cinnamon, Orris Root, Rosemary, Liquorice, Black Peppercorn, Manuka Honey & Ginger

TASTING NOTES:
Intense rosemary, light pepper and ginger spice on the nose, strong ginger and garden herbs with peppery heat on the palate, a touch of honey with rosemary and pepper to finish.

SERVING SUGGESTION:
Enjoy with Fever-Tree Premium Indian Tonic Water.

Lavender Hill Sloe Gin

33% ABV

A sloe gin, Lavender Hill Sloe Gin is a limited edition made using sloe berries from their farm steeped for three months in a gin made with 14 botanicals, giving it a dark inky red colour.

DISTILLERY:
Lavender Hill, Riverhead

BOTANICALS:
Juniper, Coriander Seed, Cassia, Angelica Root, Nutmeg, Citrus Peel, Tangerine, Orris Root, Star Anise, Anise, Lemon, Orange & Cardamom (Steeped in Sloe Berries for three months)

TASTING NOTES:
Acidic plum, raw almond, and a touch of fresh hay on the nose, dark acidic blackcurrant with a hay and green almond note on the palate, tart acidic fruit driven finish.

SERVING SUGGESTION:
Enjoy with Fever-Tree Premium Indian Tonic Water.

Lavender Hill & Bees Up Top Smoked Honey Gin
40% ABV

A flavoured gin, Lavender Hill & Bees Up Top Smoked Honey Gin is a collaboration that blends their gin with lavender honey direct from their farm and added notes from the beekeepers smoke, imparting a cloudy pale yellow colour.

DISTILLERY:
Lavender Hill, Riverhead

BOTANICALS:
Juniper, Coriander Seed, Cassia, Angelica Root, Nutmeg, Citrus Peel, Tangerine, Orris Root, Star Anise, Anise, Lemon, Orange, Cardamom & Honey

TASTING NOTES:
Floral honey with a delicate touch of smoke on the nose, coriander and orris root accented by honey and light smoke on the palate, raw honey continues to finish.

SERVING SUGGESTION:
Enjoy with Fever-Tree Premium Indian Tonic Water.

The Racketeer Blackcurrant Gin
27% ABV

A flavoured gin, The Racketeer Blackcurrant Gin is made by soaking blackcurrants from their back garden in their London Dry Gin and then sweetened with a homemade sugar syrup, with a deep purple-red colour.

DISTILLERY:
Longshot Distillery, Rolleston

BOTANICALS:
Juniper, Coriander Seed, Almond, Lemon, Orange, Elderberry, Rosehip & Blackcurrant

TASTING NOTES:
Unmistakable blackcurrant with hints of marzipan on the nose, tart acidic blackcurrant, light orange and some spice on the palate, slightly tannic off-dry finish.

SERVING SUGGESTION:
Enjoy with Fever-Tree Refreshingly Light Indian Tonic Water.

The Racketeer Plum Gin
40% ABV

A flavoured gin, The Racketeer Plum Gin uses their London Dry Gin as its base, then soaked in plums from their own trees and sweetened with a homemade sugar syrup, with a wine red colour.

DISTILLERY:
LongShot Distillery, Rolleston

BOTANICALS:
Juniper, Coriander Seed, Almond, Lemon, Orange, Elderberry, Rosehip & Plum

TASTING NOTES:
Tart red fruits, marzipan character with a citrus lift on the nose, bitter red fruits with a hint of florals and oily orange on the palate, drying citrus and red fruits to finish.

SERVING SUGGESTION:
Enjoy with Fever-Tree Refreshingly Light Indian Tonic Water.

NDC Adorn Rosé Beauty Gin

42% ABV

A flavoured gin, NDC Adorn Rosé Beauty Gin is inspired by the botanicals found in luxury New Zealand skincare products including New Zealand flax seed, rose petals, organic rosehip, and chamomile, with a dark pink colour.

DISTILLERY:
The National Distillery Co., Napier

BOTANICALS:
Juniper, Coriander Seed, Angelica Root, Cardamom, Orris Root, Cassia, Lemon Peel, Rosehip, Rose Petal, Chamomile, Flax Seed & Liquorice Root

TASTING NOTES:
Earthy florals, cassia, and dry hay like chamomile on the nose, earthy spice with supporting rose and chamomile lead the palate, hot spice with lingering earthiness to finish.

SERVING SUGGESTION:
Enjoy with Fever-Tree Elderflower Tonic Water.

No8 Distillery Moka Gin
38% ABV

A flavoured gin, No8 Distillery Moka Gin is a collaboration with Vanguard Specialty Coffee Company and Ocho Chocolate to make a 'Breakfast Gin' with three waves of cold brew coffee, chocolate, and citrus.

DISTILLERY:
No8 Distillery, Dunedin

BOTANICALS:
Juniper, Coffee Husk, Cocoa Husk, Orange, Cardamom & Pink Pepper (infused with Ethiopian Coffee Beans)

TASTING NOTES:
Warming orange and cardamom with a dusting of dark chocolate and coffee grounds on the nose, mocha to open with brewed coffee on the palate, persistent cardamom and orange to finish.

SERVING SUGGESTION:
Enjoy with Fever-Tree Distillers Cola.

Rose & Twig Blood Orange Gin

37.5% ABV

A flavoured gin, Rose & Twig Blood Orange is triple distilled with six core botanicals, including ripe blood oranges, which impart it with a vibrant red-tinged orange colour.

DISTILLERY:
Premium Liquor Co., Auckland

BOTANICALS:
Juniper, Nutmeg, Angelica Root, Orange, Tangerine, Coriander Seed, Cardamom, Lemon, Mandarin, Grapefruit & Clementine

TASTING NOTES:
Sweet orange and bitter pith on the nose, slightly astringent citrus with some earthy support form on the palate, a sweet confectionary driven finish.

SERVING SUGGESTION:
Enjoy with Fever-Tree Blood Orange Soda.

Premium
LIQUOR CO.

Rose & Twig Blueberry Gin
37.5% ABV

A flavoured gin, Rose & Twig Blueberry Gin is triple distilled with six core botanicals, including blueberries which give it a rich indigo colour.

DISTILLERY:
Premium Liquor Co., Auckland

BOTANICALS:
Juniper, Nutmeg, Angelica Root, Orange, Tangerine, Coriander Seed, Cardamom, Lemon, Mandarin, Grapefruit & Clementine

TASTING NOTES:
Pronounced blueberry extract with light earth on the nose, astringent berry and sweetness on the palate, a touch of root spice lead a drying finish.

SERVING SUGGESTION:
Enjoy with Fever-Tree Wild Raspberry Tonic Water.

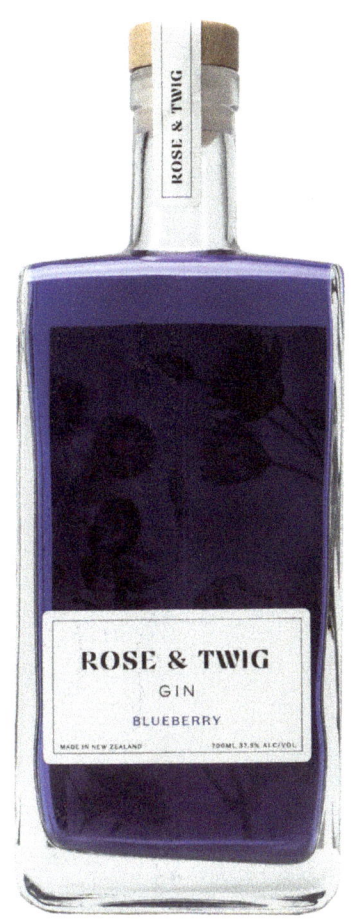

Rose & Twig Pomegranate Gin

37.5% ABV

A flavoured gin, Rose & Twig Pomegranate Gin is triple distilled with six core botanicals and infused with pomegranate juice, which imparts a delicate pink colour.

DISTILLERY:
Premium Liquor Co., Auckland

BOTANICALS:
Juniper, Nutmeg, Angelica Root, Orange, Tangerine, Coriander Seed, Cardamom, Lemon, Mandarin, Grapefruit & Clementine

TASTING NOTES:
Caramelised citrus peel and root spice on the nose, red fruit and root spice lead the palate, sweet fruits drive a hot finish.

SERVING SUGGESTION:
Enjoy with Fever-Tree Refreshingly Light Indian Tonic Water.

Sundown Black Doris Plum Gin

40% ABV

A flavoured gin, Sundown Black Doris Plum Gin is inspired by the natural beauty of New Zealand, blending traditional botanicals with natural Black Doris plum flavour and water from the Tautau and Waiorohi streams.

DISTILLERY:
Premium Liquor Co., Auckland

BOTANICALS:
Juniper, Coriander Seed, Orris Root, Angelica Root, Citrus Peel & Black Doris Plum

TASTING NOTES:
Intense sweet plum cordial on the nose, floral plum with distinct sweetness drives the palate, rich plum sweetness fades in to the finish.

SERVING SUGGESTION:
Enjoy with Fever-Tree Refreshingly Light Indian Tonic Water.

Premium
LIQUOR CO.

Sundown Grapefruit & Elderflower Gin
40% ABV

A flavoured gin, Sundown Grapefruit & Elderflower Gin is inspired by the natural beauty of Aotearoa, blending traditional botanicals with natural grapefruit and elderflower extracts, and water from the Tautau and Waiorohi streams.

DISTILLERY:
Premium Liquor Co., Auckland

BOTANICALS:
Juniper, Coriander Seed, Orris Root, Angelica Root, Citrus Peel, Grapefruit & Elderflower

TASTING NOTES:
Bright floral grapefruit on the nose, sharp orange and grapefruit with confectionary-like florals on the palate, persistent grapefruit and lingering florals to finish.

SERVING SUGGESTION:
Enjoy with Fever-Tree Elderflower Tonic Water.

PREMIUM SPIRITS
REEFTON DISTILLING CO.
WEST COAST—NEW ZEALAND
ESTD 2017

Little Biddy Gin - Hazy Spiced Apple
40% ABV

A flavoured gin, Little Biddy Gin Hazy Spiced Apple is designed to express the warm and familiar aroma and taste of fresh apple pie, with apple juice, apple mint, ginger, and nutmeg amongst its botanicals.

DISTILLERY:
Reefton Distilling Co., Reefton

BOTANICALS:
Juniper, Apple Juice, Apple Mint, Tarata, Ginger, Nutmeg, Allspice, Angelica Root, Cardamom, Cassia, Coriander Seed, Liquorice & Orris Root

TASTING NOTES:
Funky stewed apple, bold baking spice and a grassy note on the nose, apple sweetness with cardamom rounded out by strong baking spice on the palate, apple crumble-like finish with crushed mint.

SERVING SUGGESTION:
Enjoy with Fever-Tree Ginger Beer.

SOLACE GIN

Solace Raspberry & Cranberry Gin
37.5% ABV

A flavoured gin, Solace Raspberry & Cranberry Gin uses their London Dry Gin as a base and is then sweetened with natural berry extracts, which give it a deep pink colour.

DISTILLERY:
Kings Liquor, Auckland

BOTANICALS:
Juniper, Coriander Seed, Cassia, Angelica Root, Nutmeg, Citrus Peel, Tangerine, Orris Root, Star Anise, Anise, Lemon, Orange, Cardamom & Natural Berry Extract

TASTING NOTES:
Sweet candied berries and lemon on the nose, sweet berry supported by anise and liquorice on the palate, sweet driven finish.

SERVING SUGGESTION:
Enjoy with Fever-Tree Wild Raspberry Tonic Water.

Victor Gin Blanc De Blancs
42% ABV

A flavoured gin, Victor Gin Blanc De Blancs is made from a marriage between the botanicals in their Heavy Botanical gin and chardonnay grape juice from their local region.

DISTILLERY:
Thomson Whisky Distillery, Riverhead

BOTANICALS:
Juniper, Lemon, Lemongrass, Cardamom, Coriander Seed & Chardonnay Grape Juice

TASTING NOTES:
Candied lemongrass, lemon sorbet and sweet grapes on the nose, sweet lemon, coriander and hints of baked apricot on the palate, slightly sweet-fruity finish.

SERVING SUGGESTION:
Enjoy with Fever-Tree Mediterranean Tonic Water.

Waiheke Distilling Co. Red Ruby Gin
42% ABV

A flavoured gin, Waiheke Distilling Co. Ruby Red Gin is the 'jewel' in their collection, infused with sweet New Zealand cherries and boasting a luscious red colour.

DISTILLERY:
Waiheke Distilling Co., Waiheke

BOTANICALS:
Juniper & Others

TASTING NOTES:
Sweet cherry with lime and clove on the nose, baking spice leads with rich sweet red fruit on the palate, drying sweetness with a resinous oily finish.

SERVING SUGGESTION:
Enjoy with Fever-Tree Premium Indian Tonic Water.

Waitoki Washhouse

Washhouse Fresh Rhubarb Gin

43% ABV

A flavoured gin, Waitoki Washhouse Gin with Fresh Rhubarb is distilled with a blend of traditional and native New Zealand botanicals which is then steeped in locally grown rhubarb, giving it a rich pink colour.

DISTILLERY:
Washhouse Distillery, Waitoki

BOTANICALS:
Juniper, Coriander Seed, Angelica Root, Rhubarb, Grapefruit, Orange, Kawakawa & Horopito

TASTING NOTES:
Slight strawberry character with bitter rhubarb and kawakawa on the nose, juniper leads with rhubarb tartness and a growing kawakawa note on the palate, heated horopito spice leads the finish.

SERVING SUGGESTION:
Enjoy with Fever-Tree Wild Raspberry Tonic Water.

WHITE SHEEP CO.

New Zealand

White Sheep Co. Sheep Milk & Honey

42% ABV

A flavoured gin, White Sheep Co.'s Sheep Milk & Honey Gin uses a fermented sheep's milk spirit and includes premium local honey among its botanicals which evokes the idea of New Zealand being a 'land of milk and honey' and imparts a golden hue.

DISTILLERY:
The White Sheep Co., Whangamata

BOTANICALS:
Juniper, Manuka Honey, Angelica Root, Orris Root, Clementine Zest, Coriander Seed, Lemon Zest & Allspice

TASTING NOTES:
Gentle spice, citrus and honey on the nose, creamed clover honey, root spice and pepper lead the palate, soft velvety finish.

SERVING SUGGESTION:
Enjoy with Fever-Tree Premium Lemonade.

WILD DIAMOND

Wild Diamond Feijoa Gin

42% ABV

A flavoured gin, Wild Diamond Feijoa Gin is a limited edition that uses their Rare Dry Gin as the base with an extra infusion of organic feijoa, which gives it a soft golden colour.

DISTILLERY:
Wild Diamond Distillery, Queenstown

BOTANICALS:
Juniper, Coriander Seed, Angelica Root, Cassia, Liquorice Extract, Cinnamon, Almond, Feijoa & Others

TASTING NOTES:
Slightly astringent feijoa, apple, and citrus on the nose, light fruit with bold spice on the palate, mellowing spice with subtle fruit to finish.

SERVING SUGGESTION:
Enjoy with Fever-Tree Refreshingly Light Indian Tonic Water.

Wild Diamond Saffron Gin
42% ABV

A flavoured gin, Wild Diamond Saffron Gin is a limited edition that uses their Rare Dry Gin as the base with an extra infusion of locally grown Lake Hawea saffron, which gives it a bright yellow colour.

DISTILLERY:
Wild Diamond Distillery, Queenstown

BOTANICALS:
Juniper, Coriander Seed, Angelica Root, Cassia, Liquorice Extract, Cinnamon, Almond, Saffron & Others

TASTING NOTES:
Earthy root tones with lime on the nose, juniper and spice lead with subtle saffron on the palate, mellowing honey to finish.

SERVING SUGGESTION:
Enjoy with Fever-Tree Refreshingly Light Indian Tonic Water.

WILD DIAMOND

Wild Diamond Vanilla Gin
42% ABV

A flavoured gin, Wild Diamond Vanilla Gin is a limited edition that uses their Rare Dry Gin as the base, with an extra infusion of organic vanilla, which gives it a pale golden colour.

DISTILLERY:
Wild Diamond Distillery, Queenstown

BOTANICALS:
Juniper, Coriander Seed, Angelica Root, Cassia, Liquorice Extract, Cinnamon, Almond, Vanilla & Others

TASTING NOTES:
Soft florals with hints of vanilla and cassia on the nose, peppery spice with cinnamon and liquorice on the palate, earthy spice lingering on the finish.

SERVING SUGGESTION:
Enjoy with Fever-Tree Premium Indian Tonic Water.

AGED

AGED GIN

Gin rested for a noted period of time. Generally influenced by wood, rested in a tank with staves or woodchips, or matured in a barrel or cask.

Awildian Manuka Gin
47% ABV

An aged gin, Awildian Manuka Gin is rested in toasted Manuka wood coated with medicinal grade Manuka honey for no less than 3 months, which imparts a pale golden colour.

DISTILLERY:
Coromandel Distilling Co., Thames

BOTANICALS:
Juniper, Coriander Seed, Cassia, Cinnamon, Chamomile, Grains of Paradise, Seville Orange, English Lavender, Vanilla, Cardamom, Ginger, Madagascan Pepper, Manuka Honey & Others

MATURATION:
Rested for Three months in Manuka Wood

TASTING NOTES:
Green and fresh Manuka, bush mint and menthol spice on the nose, sweet orange, ginger and pepper on the palate, a warming citrus and woody finish.

SERVING SUGGESTION:
Enjoy neat or with Fever-Tree Ginger Ale.

Broken Heart Barrel Aged Gin

40% ABV

A barrel aged gin that spends six months in French chardonnay oak barrels, Broken Heart Barrel Aged Gin is warm and welcoming with a delicate golden hue.

DISTILLERY:
Broken Heart Spirits, Arrow Junction

BOTANICALS:
Juniper, Coriander Seed, Lavender, Angelica Root, Citrus, Orange Flower, Hops, Ginger, Pimento & Cinnamon

MATURATION:
Rested for Six months in French Chardonnay Barrels

TASTING NOTES:
Juniper, oak and coriander on the nose, slightly sweet oakiness with lavender and subtle juniper on the palate, lingering florals and light oak on the finish.

SERVING SUGGESTION:
Enjoy neat or with Fever-Tree Ginger Ale.

Curiosity Gin - Negroni Special
55% ABV

A barrel aged gin, Curiosity Gin Negroni Special is rested in new French oak barrels and designed to complement a Negroni cocktail, with a soft golden hue.

DISTILLERY:
The Spirits Workshop Distillery, Christchurch

BOTANICALS:
Juniper, Coriander Seed, Orange Zest, Lime Zest, Ginger, Angelica Root, Lavender, Cinnamon, Cardamom & Star Anise

MATURATION:
Rested for Six to Eight weeks in new French Oak Barrels

TASTING NOTES:
French oak, fennel and aniseed on the nose, rich orange zest and classic gin spice on the palate, dry bitter ginger and fennel to finish.

SERVING SUGGESTION:
Enjoy with Fever-Tree Premium Indian Tonic Water.

Dancing Sands Barrel Aged Gin

48% ABV

A barrel aged gin, Dancing Sands Barrel Aged Gin is blended from gin rested in two different barrels, one in ex-rum barrels to impart sweetness and the other in new French oak barrels for oakiness.

DISTILLERY:
Dancing Sands Distillery, Takaka

BOTANICALS:
Juniper, Coriander Seed, Peppercorn, Manuka Leaf, Almond, Liquorice, Angelica Root & Cardamom

MATURATION:
Rested for Three months in ex-Murderer's Bay Gold Rum Barrels and new French Oak Barrels

TASTING NOTES:
Rich vanilla and toffee combine with citrus on the nose, fruity raisin with a pronounced rum influence and well integrated juniper on the palate, lingering sweet fruits and juniper carry to finish.

SERVING SUGGESTION:
Enjoy neat or with Fever-Tree Ginger Ale.

ELSEWHERE

TRIPLE GIN — HAND CRAFTED

Elsewhere Fox River Triple Gin
42% ABV

A barrel aged gin, Elsewhere Fox River Triple Gin is made with botanicals from the West Coast which are blended and then aged in French oak barrels to express the wild and rugged character of the river it is named for.

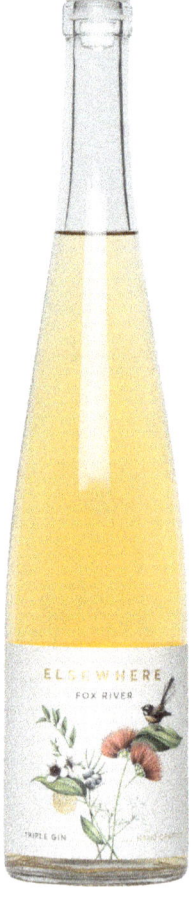

DISTILLERY:
Elsewhere Gin, Christchurch

BOTANICALS:
Juniper, Coriander Seed, Angelica Root, Lemon, Liquorice, Rata, Purple Thistle Flower, Nasturtium, Manuka Blossom, Kawakawa Fruit, Wakame Seaweed & Beach Pebble

MATURATION:
Aged in French Oak Barrels

TASTING NOTES:
Fruity and floral underpinned with baking spice on the nose, sweet liquorice, light pine and kawakawa are accented by a caramel undertone on the palate, light liquorice and pepper to finish.

SERVING SUGGESTION:
Enjoy with Fever-Tree Mediterranean Tonic Water.

Fenton Street Gin The Pioneer
46% ABV

An aged gin, Fenton Street Gin The Pioneer was made to reflect the efforts of the early European settlers that came to New Zealand by taking the barrel to the gin, rather than the gin to the barrel.

DISTILLERY:
Fenton Street Distillery, Stratford

BOTANICALS:
Juniper, Coriander Seed, Cassia, Ginger, Kawakawa, Tarata, Angelica Root, Lemon Zest, Horopito, Peppercorn, Bush Honey, Manuka & Nutmeg

MATURATION:
Not Disclosed

TASTING NOTES:
Spiced tannins, vanilla and bush honey on the nose, slightly sweet pepper and nutmeg on the palate, subtle citrus and a peppery damp green finish.

SERVING SUGGESTION:
Enjoy with Fever-Tree Ginger Ale.

I.F. (Ignis Fatuus) Gin

47% ABV

An aged gin, Hastings Distillers I.F. (Ignis Fatuus) / Gin is made using grape-based spirit and botanicals designed to evoke the ancient Kauri forests and the story of the Dalmatian gum diggers who came to New Zealand and then turn their hand to wine.

VOL. 3 — TASTERS' PICK — GUIDE TO NEW ZEALAND GIN

DISTILLERY:
Hasting Distillers, Hastings

BOTANICALS:
Juniper, Green Cardamom, Black Cardamom, Clove, Kawakawa Fruit, Kauri Gum, Kauri Oak & Others

MATURATION:
Base spirit aged prior to distillation, and gin rested 18 Months post distillation.

TASTING NOTES:
Aromatic camphor wood with fragrant kauri sap and striking menthol on the nose, scented tree florals with bold eucalyptus, clove and a slightly phenolic note on the palate, pine resin with developing florals and spice to finish.

SERVING SUGGESTION:
Enjoy neat.

Humdinger Bourbon Barrel Aged Gin
44.9% ABV

A barrel aged gin, Humdinger Bourbon Barrel Aged Gin is a limited release made by resting a blend of their Dry and Citrus Gins in an ex-bourbon barrel for three months to impart bourbon and oak notes.

DISTILLERY:
Humdinger Distillery, Geraldine

BOTANICALS:
Juniper, Barley, Coriander Seed, Nutmeg, Liquorice, Angelica Root, Ginger, Lemon Peel & Orange Peel

MATURATION:
Rested for Three months in ex-Bourbon American Oak Barrels

TASTING NOTES:
Bright lemon and orange peel on the nose, lemon and orange continue with coriander in support on the palate, ginger spice lingers with mellowing coriander and citrus to finish.

SERVING SUGGESTION:
Enjoy neat or with Fever-Tree Ginger Ale.

Black Barn Syrah Barrel Aged Gin

44.2% ABV

A barrel aged gin, imagination Black Barn Syrah Barrel Aged New Zealand Gin is made with their highest quality triple distilled gin and matured in lightly toasted French oak barrels, giving it a dusky pink colour.

DISTILLERY:
imagination, Reikorangi

BOTANICALS:
Juniper, Coriander Seed, Cinnamon, Liquorice, Orris Root, Orange, Lime, Lemon & Manuka

MATURATION:
Rested in toasted ex-Syrah French Oak Barrels

TASTING NOTES:
Rich berries and tannins on the nose, earthy liquorice, orris root and spice on the palate, mellowing earth and citrus sweetness to finish.

SERVING SUGGESTION:
Enjoy neat or with Fever-Tree Ginger Ale.

JUNO GIN
Styx Barrel-Aged Gin
55% ABV

A barrel aged gin, Styx Barrel-Aged Gin is a limited edition collaboration with artist Phil 'Suspect' Jones who has individually decorated each bottle, named for the mythical Greek goddess and underworld river.

DISTILLERY:
Begin Distilling, New Plymouth

BOTANICALS:
Juniper, Coriander Seed, Angelica Root, Orris Root, Cassia, Orange, Cardamom, Nutmeg, Manuka, Makrut Lime Leaf & Black Peppercorn

MATURATION:
Rested in ex-Port French Oak Barrels

TASTING NOTES:
Light oak with vibrant juniper, light honey and spice botanicals on the nose, juniper, coriander and angelica accented by a sweet vanilla tone on the palate, touches of spice with lasting angelica to finish.

SERVING SUGGESTION:
Enjoy neat or with Fever-Tree Ginger Ale.

Guide to New Zealand Gin — Vol. 3 — Tasters' Pick

Gin & Bare It Ginisky

40% ABV

An aged gin, Gin & Bare It Ginisky is a limited release designed to be enjoyed as a sipping gin by incorporating the qualities of both whisky and gin, with a golden hue.

DISTILLERY:
Lammermoor Distillery, Lammermoor

BOTANICALS:
Juniper & Others

MATURATION:
Not Disclosed

TASTING NOTES:
Notes of lemonade citrus and coriander on the nose, sweet dried fruits with lemon and orange oil on the palate, lemon and dried fruit character carry with a touch of spice to finish.

SERVING SUGGESTION:
Enjoy neat or with Fever-Tree Ginger Ale.

Lighthouse Barrel Aged Gin
45% ABV

A barrel aged gin, Lighthouse Gin Barrel Aged Gin was perfected over the course of four years using their same blend of nine botanicals, which is then rested in ex-pinot noir barrels from a Martinborough vineyard, giving it an oaky amber hue.

DISTILLERY:
Lighthouse Gin Distillery, Martinborough

BOTANICALS:
Juniper, Coriander Seed, Yen Ben Lemon Zest, Navel Orange Zest, Cinnamon, Almond, Cassia, Orris Root & Liquorice

MATURATION:
Rested in ex-Pinot Noir Barrels

TASTING NOTES:
Citrus and nuttiness with hints of caramel on the nose, upfront coriander with a strong juniper backbone accented by balanced oak on the palate, mellowing pepper and baking spice to finish.

SERVING SUGGESTION:
Enjoy neat or with Fever-Tree Ginger Ale.

Woodcutter Barrel Aged Gin

41% ABV

A barrel aged gin, Sandymount Distillery Woodcutter Barrel Aged Gin is inspired by the native bush tracks and pine forests on the distillery's grounds, with a pale sandy gold colour.

DISTILLERY:
Sandymount Distillery, Otago Peninsula

BOTANICALS:
Juniper, Coriander Seed, Cardamom, Angelica Root, Orris Root, Cinnamon, Lemon & Orange

MATURATION:
Rested in ex-Pinot Noir Oak Barrels

TASTING NOTES:
Characterful steeped fruits with a touch of saw dust on the nose, creamy-buttery botanicals with warming orange and cinnamon on the palate, buttery botanical tones fade quickly to finish.

SERVING SUGGESTION:
Enjoy neat or with Fever-Tree Ginger Ale.

Waitoki Washhouse

Waitoki Washhouse Barrel Aged Gin

43% ABV

A barrel aged gin, Waitoki Washhouse Gin Barrel Aged is made by resting their original gin in ex-chardonnay French oak barrels from a winery in the Ararimu Valley northwest of Auckland.

DISTILLERY:
Washhouse Distillery, Waitoki

BOTANICALS:
Juniper, Coriander Seed, Angelica Root, Grapefruit, Orange, Kawakawa & Horopito

MATURATION:
Rested in ex-Chardonnay French Oak Barrels

TASTING NOTES:
Pronounced kawakawa and grapefruit with a slight phenolic note on the nose, sweet kawakawa with strong horopito pepper on the palate, heat levels off with a touch of kawakawa to finish.

SERVING SUGGESTION:
Enjoy neat or with Fever-Tree Ginger Ale.

ALCOHOL-FREE SPIRIT

ALCOHOL-FREE SPIRIT

Distilled without the presence of alcohol.

BROKEN HEART
——— GIN ———
Distilled in the Pure South of New Zealand

Broken Heart 0% Alcohol Botanical Spirit
ALCOHOL FREE SPIRIT

A non-alcoholic spirit, Broken Heart 0% Alcohol Botanical Spirit is designed to be reminiscent of their original gin with a twist for those that want to try it but don't want the alcohol.

DISTILLERY:
Broken Heart Spirits, Arrow Junction

BOTANICALS:
Juniper, Lemon, Orange Blossom, Lavender & Ginger

TASTING NOTES:
Ginger and orange with striking lavender on the nose, florals lead with predominant lavender on the palate, touch of bitter citrus with florals to finish.

SERVING SUGGESTION:
Enjoy with Fever-Tree Premium Indian Tonic Water.

ECOLOGY + CO
FOR ALCOHOL-FREE SPIRITS

Ecology & Co. Asian Spice
Alcohol Free Spirit

A non-alcoholic spirit, Ecology & Co. Asian Spice Distilled Alcohol-Free Spirit is made using a variety of herbs and spices from across Asia and elsewhere, aimed at those with an adventurous or evolved palette.

DISTILLERY:
Ecology & Co., Auckland

BOTANICALS:
Juniper, Coriander Seed, Lavender, Mint, Chamomile, Lemon Verbena, Orris Root, Thyme, Rosemary, Lime Peel, Kelp, Horopito & Bay Leaf

TASTING NOTES:
Spice driven aromatics on the nose, light and clean spice on the palate, cardamom carries through to the finish.

SERVING SUGGESTION:
Enjoy with Fever-Tree Refreshingly Light Indian Tonic Water.

ECOLOGY+CO
FOR ALCOHOL-FREE SPIRITS

Ecology & Co. London Dry
ALCOHOL FREE SPIRIT

A non-alcoholic spirit, Ecology & Co. London Dry Distilled Alcohol-Free Spirit focuses on a traditional blend of gin botanicals to create a zero percent replacement for the gin in a classic G&T.

DISTILLERY:
Ecology & Co., Auckland

BOTANICALS:
Cardamom, Black Peppercorn, Cassia, Basil, Cumin & Lemon Myrtle

TASTING NOTES:
Citrus and bitter peel on the nose, light spice with bitter citrus on the palate, astringent drive to finish.

SERVING SUGGESTION:
Enjoy with Fever-Tree Refreshingly Light Indian Tonic Water.

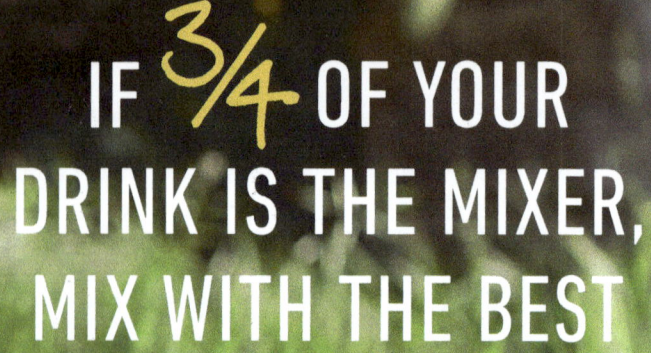

A SHORT HISTORY OF TONIC

NO CARBONATION, NO TONIC. NO TONIC, NO FEVER-TREE!
Does not bear thinking about. We have gin, we have ice and now we have carbonation. But what about tonic?

To find the answer to that question you only have to look at the name itself. You see, unlike gin, tonic really does have medicinal qualities to it. Or at least, quinine which is found in the bark of the Cinchona Tree from which Tonic is made does (and just as well too). In the 1600's, with the world plagued by malaria carrying mosquitos, a Jesuit monk called Agostino (Jesuits were considered the geniuses of the time) discovered that native Indians who would chew the Cinchona bark when they had fever would see their fever subside.

So, he wondered whether it could do the same with Malaria – and hey presto! The medicine was sent all over Europe and for the first time ever there was a way to prevent the epidemic spreading.

In the 1800s, we saw the first 'Indian Tonic Waters' created as the British soldiers stationed in India mixed their daily ration of quinine with 'a spoonful of sugar to help the medicine go down' along with some local spices and citrus. That little Cinchona bark pretty much changed the world. These enterprising soldiers and their counter parts in the Royal Navy couldn't resist mixing this medicinal mixture with their ration of gin. The humble G&T. This little concoction revolutionised the way people took their daily medicine and also when they took it. With the mosquitos choosing to come out as the sun went down, all over Europe people would raise a glass at sunset and enjoy a gin and tonic as a pleasantly social ritual.

In London, gin's reputation was on the rise. So much was gin's transformation that it inspired one London-based gentleman, an Erasmus Bond, to come up with the simple, yet wonderful idea of a pre-made tonic. In doing so, the social status of the drink had now been well and truly elevated.

DID YOU KNOW?
Under a UV light, the quinine in tonic water makes the water fluoresce a brilliant bright blue.

SIR WINSTON CHURCHILL SAID...
"Gin and tonic has saved more Englishmen's lives, and minds, than all the doctors in the Empire!"

HOW TO CREATE THE
PERFECT GIN & TONIC

It all began in 2003 with a meeting of minds and one simple premise: if three quarters of your G&T is the tonic, wouldn't you want it to be the best?

REIGNITING A LONG-FORGOTTEN AND NEGLECTED SECTOR OF THE DRINKS INDUSTRY

Our co-founders Charles and Tim, working in different parts of the drinks business, had both spotted that premium spirits were growing quickly, fuelled by consumers' increasing awareness of the provenance of what they ate and drank.

However, this growing interest in premium food and drink had seemed to neglect mixers, a crucial element of the drinks industry that remained flat. It struck them both as extraordinary that people were paying a good deal of money for a high-quality spirit, yet had no choice but drown it with a poor-quality mixer

CHARLES AND TIM SET OUT TO PUT QUALITY BACK INTO MIXERS

From the very beginning, Charles and Tim approached their business in a different way – there would be no compromise at Fever-Tree. Flavour and quality were of the utmost importance. This mindset led them on an 18-month adventure from the archives of the British Library to facing the wrong end of a Kalashnikov in the Democratic Republic of Congo and concluded with the launch of our Premium Indian Tonic Water in 2005, with the belief we still operate by today…

PIONEERING TO PRODUCE AN UNRIVALLED DRINKING EXPERIENCE AT EVERY OCCASION

Since we put the lid on our first bottle of our Premium Indian Tonic Water, we haven't wavered in our single-minded mission to bring quality, flavour and choice back to mixers. Innovation remains at the heart of Fever-Tree and we've developed an award winning range of tonic waters that perfectly complement the varied flavour categories of gin. We've found three incredibly diverse varieties of ginger that, together, create a remarkably deep, fresh and true taste, which we've used to make a selection of ginger ales and ginger beer. We have lemonades using the finest, naturally sourced ingredients and have recently launched our Soda

Collection – A brand-new range of three mouth-watering flavoured sodas, including Lime & Yuzu, Italian Blood Orange and Pink Grapefruit. Our story is about going to the ends of the earth in pursuit of the best and, the most exciting thing is, we've only just scratched the surface.

OUR MIXERS
We start with the idea that, if ¾ of your drink is the mixer, then you should use the best. We work with only the best naturally sourced ingredients from around the world and no artificial flavourings or sweeteners to create mixers that do justice to the world's finest spirits

PAIR YOUR FAVOURITE PREMIUM GINS WITH FEVER-TREE MIXERS

Gin is an often overlooked spirit, despite its incredibly rich diversity. Bursts of juicy citrus, deliciously savoury herb notes and crisp, floral flavours are just some of the immense range of characteristics this one spirit can contain. Fever-Tree has been on a relentless pioneering pursuit to create a selection of award-winning tonic waters, each one individually crafted to complement the diverse flavour profiles of gin. While made with gins in mind, our tonics pair equally as well.

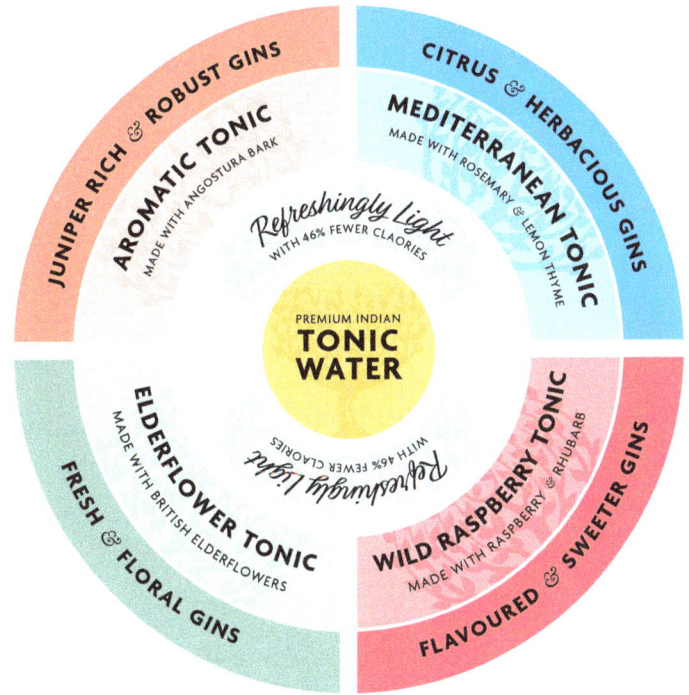

TONICS

PREMIUM INDIAN TONIC WATER

By blending subtle botanicals flavours with spring water and quinine of the highest quality from the fever trees of the Democratic Republic of the Congo, we have created a delicious tonic water with a uniquely refreshing taste and aroma.

REFRESHINGLY LIGHT INDIAN TONIC WATER

We use naturally occurring fruit sugars to develop our lighter tonic water. The blending of subtle botanical flavours with spring water and highest-quality quinine gives it the distinctively clean, crisp character of Indian Tonic Water, but with 46% fewer calories.

MEDITERRANEAN TONIC WATER

By blending the essential oils from the flowers, fruits and herbs that we have gathered from around the Mediterranean shores with the quinine of the highest quality from the fever trees of the Democratic Republic of the Congo, we have created a delicious, delicate, floral tonic water.

REFRESHINGLY LIGHT MEDITERRANEAN TONIC WATER

With 46% fewer calories than our regular Mediterranean Tonic Water, we use fruit sugars to develop our lighter tonic water, meaning its delicious and low in calories. Contains natural flavours and no artificial sweeteners.

AROMATIC TONIC WATER

By blending the gentle bitterness of South American angostura bark with aromatic botanicals such as cardamom, pimento berry and ginger, we've created a delicious, unique tonic water that can be enjoyed in a Pink G&T or as a sophisticated soft drink on its own.

ELDERFLOWER TONIC WATER

By blending the essential oils from handpicked English elderflowers with quinine of the highest quality from the fever trees of the Democratic Republic of the Congo, we have created a delicious, floral variation of our Indian Tonic Water.

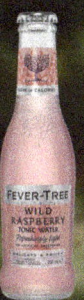

WILD RASPBERRY TONIC WATER

By blending natural flavourings of juicy Scottish raspberries with sweet rhubarb, we've created a refreshingly fruity tonic water, reminiscent of summer. Simply mix with your favourite pink or London Dry Gin for a sweeter twist on a gin and tonic.

GINGERS & COLA

PREMIUM GINGER BEER

A brewed product that contains a unique blend of the finest gingers, subtle botanical flavours and spring water. Not too sweet on the palate and with a deep long lasting ginger character.

DRY GINGER ALE

By using a unique blend of naturally sourced gingers, subtle botanical flavours and spring water, we have created a delicious Ginger Ale with an authentic, refreshing taste and aroma. Perfectly balanced to enhance the flavour notes of the finest whiskies, bourbons and rums.

DISTILLERS COLA

Our recipe is no secret. We are proud to use a selection of the finest naturally sourced ingredients including Caribbean kola nuts, Tahitian limes and a selection of distilled botanicals & spices including Jamaican pimento berry & Madagascan vanilla

SODAS

ITALIAN BLOOD ORANGE SODA

Juicy blood oranges from Sicily meet an iconic herbal blend to create our Italian Blood Orange Soda. This complex and sophisticated mixer pairs perfectly with Italian liqueurs, bitters and premium vodka.

LIME & YUZU SODA

Our Lime & Yuzu Soda is made with Tahiti lime from Mexico's fertile groves in addition to pressed juice from the wonderfully floral Japanese yuzu, to create a low-calorie soda that's perfect for mixing with premium vodka or tequila for a mouth wateringly zesty summer spritz.

PINK GRAPEFRUIT SODA

This delicious, low-calorie soda is made with real juice from hand-picked pink Florida grapefruits. Pairs perfectly with tequila or mezcal for a classic Paloma or with vodka for a refreshing, light spritz. Less than half the calories & sugar of traditional grapefruit juice or other grapefruit sodas.

PREMIUM SODA WATER

By using soft spring water, bicarbonate of soda and a high level of carbonation, we have created a delicious soda water with a delicate aroma. Perfect for bringing out the best flavours of the finest whiskies.

— DISTILLERY —
DIRECTORY

1919 DISTILLING, AUCKLAND
1919distilling.com

Nestled in the bustling industrial area of Auckland's East Tamaki, 1919 Distilling prides itself on sourcing everything locally, even down to their custom made still, so that they can ensure the best quality and craftsmanship. Named for the year that New Zealand voted down prohibition they also stay true to the way gin was made in the 1900's by using ethanol made from cane sugar rather than whey.

AKAROA CRAFT DISTILLERY, AKAROA
akaroacraftdistillery.com

Surrounded by the beauty of the Banks Peninsula in the heart of historic Akaroa with its French heritage, Akaroa Craft Distillery focuses on distilling the stories of the past, the land, and history while adding to it and giving back to the region. They use local ingredients in their spirits to capture the regions flavours and evoke a sense of place.

ARIKI SPIRIT, MOUNT MAUNGANUI
arikispirit.com

Tucked away in the balmy Bay of Plenty, Ariki Spirit crafts their gin using unique botanicals to achieve distinctive aromatic notes. Ariki means 'high chief' or 'leader' in Te Reo, with cognates throughout the Pacific, and is associated with carrying great prestige or mana and reflects their ambition of bringing the 'Spirit of the Pacific' to the world.

Dr Beak

ARISE SPIRITS, MARTINBOROUGH
drbeak.nz

Based in the warm micro-climate of Martinborough in the Wairarapa but distilled in Blenheim, Arise Spirits took three years of recipe development to get where they are now. Each botanical they use has been carefully selected based on their ability to be grown in New Zealand, with the aim of one day creating a gin from single site grown botanicals. With environmentalism at their core, they also donate 5% of their profits to Forest and Bird.

ARROWTOWN DISTILLERY, ARROWTOWN
riftersgin.com

Resting beneath the picturesque Coronet Peak, Arrowtown Distillery make small batches of handcrafted gin using pure artesian water. Started by two kiwi builders with a fondness for gin and an eye to sustainability, they use a selection of botanicals from the local area much like the foraging of the namesakes of their gin for nuggets during the gold rush.

AURORA DISTILLERY, LOWER HUTT
auroradistillery.co.nz

Based in the Maungaraki suburb of Lower Hutt beneath the Western Hills, Aurora Distillery embraces the blend of art and science that used in distilling and was set up with aim of making great gin and sharing that experience. They use locally gathered botanicals and New Zealand fruits to create their small batch gins and liqueurs.

BATCH10 SPIRITS, PUHOI
batch10.com

Located in the idyllic backwoods of Puhoi, batch10 Spirits was started by a bunch of mates in one of their sheds infusing premium bourbon with local native bush honey. Having grown and developed since then they now make a range of distilled spirits crafted from the finest New Zealand and international ingredients.

BEGIN DISTILLING, NEW PLYMOUTH
junogin.com

Situated in New Plymouth's suburb of Westown near the start of Surf Highway 45, BeGin Distilling is the home of Juno Gin. Following their three key values of "Make if Fun", "Make it Together", and "Make it Right" they engage with horticulturalists and researchers to locally source botanicals and show their efficacy and flavour potential.

BLACK COLLAR DISTILLERY, KERIKERI
blackcollardistillery.com

Situated in Kerikeri in the tranquil Bay of Islands, the beating heart of Black Collar Distillery is their gorgeous handmade copper pot still called 'Frankie'. Completely old school with no automation or computer programs, it's all down to the knowledge and fine tuning of the distiller to capture just the right qualities to produce their award winning gin.

BLUSH GIN, AUCKLAND
blushginstore.co.nz

Hidden amongst the urban sprawl of Auckland city, Blush Gin was born from many experiments with all sorts of spirit infusions. Their vision is to change the perception of gin from that of "Mother's Ruin" to one of a lively and pleasant drink to be enjoyed. As natural products, it is important to store their gins in a cool dark place like a fine wine in order to retain their vibrant colours.

BROKEN HEART SPIRITS, ARROW JUNCTION
brokenheartspirits.com

Nestled in the foothills of the Southern Alps near picturesque Arrowtown, Broken Heart Spirits was born from the memory of a beloved life lost. They endeavour to create gin that captures the glory days of a friendship between two Germans that met in the South Island and bonded over their mutual appreciation for creating fine spirits before one of them tragically died.

BUREAUCRATS GIN, WELLINGTON
bureaucratsgin.co.nz

Located in the windy capital city of Wellington, Bureaucrats Gin was started by two bureaucrats with a hobby of distilling gin in their home laundries. Driven by a love of fine gin and fine things they used the age old method of trial and error until they had developed distillation consistency and quality which they could share with the world. Producing small batches, they focus on innovation and bold botanical combinations.

THE CAMBRIDGE DISTILLERY CO., CAMBRIDGE
thecambridgedistillery.co.nz

Situated amongst picturesque Cambridge's leafy streets, The Cambridge Distillery Co. endeavours to produce spirits that remind you of a certain place, a terroir, a homestead. They select their botanicals to capture and convey their surroundings, many of which are foraged from around the community, distilling them in small batches with locally sourced pure New Zealand spring water.

THE CARDRONA DISTILLERY, CARDRONA
cardronadistillery.co.nz

Tucked up in the breath-taking Cardrona Valley between Wanaka and Queenstown, The Source is produced on-site at the

Cardrona Distillery. They use a single malt spirit in their two bespoke, handmade copper pot stills all the way from Scotland and abstain from chill-filter in order to achieve a fuller flavour and character.

CHEMISTRY GIN, WELLINGTON
chemistrygin.com

Huddled within the peaceful basin of Karori in western Wellington, Chemistry Gin is run as a labour of love by two women, one of whom is a medical biochemist, and the fulfilment of a long-held dream. They explored sustainably sourced botanicals at a molecular level to bring out their flavours and balance in their gin, which is bottled in recycled glass and supports women in STEM by donating $2 from every bottle.

COROMANDEL DISTILLING CO., THAMES
awildian.com

Stationed in Thames just a stone's throw from the Coromandel Forest Park and the Kauaeranga Valley where they source their water and several botanicals, Coromandel Distilling Co. produce boutique gins using a custom 150L, German-made CARL still. As members of the 1% for the Planet organisation they give 1% of their revenue to conservation to preserve the wilderness that they benefit from.

D:STIL PROJECT, COATESVILLE
dstilproject.nz

Sequestered away in the rural paradise of Coatesville just to the northwest of Auckland, d:STIL Project is a boutique distillery and gin school founded by a lover of all things botanical, from gardening to gin, who also serves as a judge at the NZ Spirit Awards. They design their gin to celebrate the local area in which they live and work, and its rural nature.

DANCING SANDS DISTILLER., TĀKAKA
dancingsands.com

Bundled away in the small town of Takaka in Tasman region's beautiful Golden Bay area, Dancing Sands Distillery sources their water from the aquifer that feeds the nearby Te Waikoropupu Springs, often regarded as the clearest spring water in the world. They make all of their gins in small 150 litre batches to allow for maximum control over quality without any automation, instead using taste, temperature, and touch to achieve their results.

DENZIEN URBAN DISTILLERY, WELLINGTON
denzien.nz

Standing in the heart of Wellington's vibrant central Te Aro suburb, Denzien Urban Distillery is an artisan gin distillery with a mission to make brazen city gins for city people. They produce small batches in their hand-made copper pot still and use distilled rainwater, all of which can be watched in person before tasting at their visitable location.

DUNEDIN CRAFT DISTILLERS, DUNEDIN
dunedincraftdistillers.nz

Set amongst the hustle and bustle of central Dunedin's waterfront, Dunedin Craft Distillers was started by two women with a shared sense of humour and care for the environment, and the aim of reducing food waste. They brew and ferment their own base spirit from surplus bread and bakery products with the equivalent of two loaves of bread going into each 500mL bottle of spirit.

DUO DISTILLERIES, ROTORUA
duogin.co.nz

Surrounded by the geothermal wonders of Rotorua, duo Distilleries was founded by two friends with a passion for distilling and a love for entertaining friends and family, and specialise in nano-distillation. They distil each botanical, locally sourced where possible, individually using customised processes and name each gin after a semi-precious gemstone that reflects its character.

ECOLOGY+CO
FOR ALCOHOL-FREE SPIRITS

ECOLOGY & CO., AUCKLAND
ecologyandco.com

Set amongst the industry and commerce of Wairau Valley on Auckland's North Shore, Ecology & Co. are a social enterprise and artisanal distiller that produces alcohol-free spirits. They strive to make flavourful and aromatic drinks that give the same fulfilling experience as other alcohol-filled favourites but are sugar-free, carb-free, fat-free, and alcohol free.

ELEMENTAL DISTILLERS, MARLBOROUGH
elementaldistillers.com

Stationed out in the fertile Wairau Plain at the heart of the Marlborough wine region, Elemental Distillers create small batches using a boutique 200L copper pot still and a sustainable neutral base spirit. They work closely with independent farmers, foragers, and cooperatives to ensure that they get the finest quality botanicals from those who know and grow them best while striving for complete transparency, going from root to cup.

ELSEWHERE
TRIPLE GIN — HAND CRAFTED

ELSEWHERE GIN, CHRISTCHURCH
elsewheregin.com

Hidden amongst the urban sprawl of Christchurch, Elsewhere Gin is a two-person team with collective experience in winemaking and design that are dedicated to crafting very small batches of premium gin following the winemaking concept of terroir. They make place-specific gins, to which they hold a personal connection, using hand-harvested botanicals from locations across New Zealand.

EXHIBIT A
(Est. 2020)

EXHIBIT A, REIKORANGI
exhibitabrand.com

Sheltered in the lush foothills of the Reikorangi Valley on the Kapiti Coast, Exhibit A is a brand that seeks inspiration in art, literature, music, scent, and nature to create things that are original, exciting, and life-enhancing. They partnered with a Modernist sculptor to make their ceramic gin bottle and with imagination to tailor-make their gin.

FENTON STREET DISTILLERY, STRATFORD
fentonartscollective.co.nz

Huddled beneath the slopes of Mt Taranaki in the town of Stratford which is full of Shakespearian references, like many of their gins, Fenton Street Distillery has grown out of its founders' restoration of their 1920s neo-classical building. They are possibly the smallest commercial distillery in New Zealand, making deliberately small 48 litre batches to achieve a genuinely handcrafted product.

FORTH LUCK DISTILLERY, CHRISTCHURCH
forthluckgin.co.nz

Situated in the hills between the Ashley River and the rural village of Cust to the northwest of Christchurch, Forth Luck Distillery was started by a group of friends passionate about seeking inspiration from the use of organically sourced, local ingredients. They distil their small batch gins six times using a vapour infusion technique to make them as smooth as possible. Zealand, making deliberately small 48 litre batches to achieve a genuinely handcrafted product.

GOOD GEORGE DISTILLERY, HAMILTON
goodgeorge.kiwi.nz

Cloistered in the industrial suburb of Frankton in Hamilton, Good George Distillery resides in the former St George's Church from which they take their name. Originally started as a brewery, they also began making hand sanitiser in early 2020 as part of Operation Helping Hands and later decided to give their stills a day off from that project and make some gin too.

GREY LYNN GIN DISTILLERY, AUCKLAND
greylynngin.com

Nestled in the charming central Auckland suburb of Grey Lynn, Grey Lynn Gin is the latest New Zealand distiller to enter the market. Started at the beginning of the year after being conceived on New Year's Eve, they've only just arrived on shelves in September this year. Handcrafted in a local garage all of their distillation, bottling, and labelling is done by hand.

HASTINGS DISTILLERS, HASTINGS
hastingsdistillers.com

Situated near the edge of central Hastings in the fertile alluvial Heretaunga Plains, Hastings Distillers was New Zealand's first organic certified producer of spirits and liqueurs. They endeavour to grow as many of their botanicals as possible in the Hawkes Bay using organic and biodynamic practices, with the belief that the region's 'terroir' imprints on all of the botanicals. Once distilled they cut to strength using spring water from the nearby Kaweka Ranges.

HERRICK CREEK DISTILLERY, CHRISTCHURCH
herrickcreek.co.nz

Positioned in the idyllic beachside suburb of New Brighton in Christchurch, Herrick Creek is a nano-distillery making a variety of spirits in small batches using local ingredients. They take their name and inspiration from the legend of the South Island Moose with the goal of providing unique spirits influenced by North American creators.

HOLLAND ROAD DISTILLERY, EUREKA
hollandroad.co.nz

Standing in the quiet farming locality of Eureka between Hamilton and Morrinsville, Holland Road Distillery take their image and inspiration from 17th Century plague doctors who used various botanicals and herbal lore in their healing practices. They use botanicals that have long been used for their protective qualities to make their gins along with locally produced organic teas, wines, honeys, and fruits.

HUMDINGER DISTILLERY, GERALDINE
humdinger.nz

Surrounded by the tapestry of the Canterbury Plains in Geraldine, Humdinger Gin Distillery take pride in the history of their building, the 'old Morrison's Garage', and hybrid still with a 50L copper pot and 3-plate column. They focus on natural products that are truly recognisable in nature and a respect for the bees that make them all possible.

IMAGINATION, REIKORANGI
imaginationgin.nz

Sheltered in the lush foothills of the Reikorangi Valley on the Kapiti Coast, imagination is housed on the original site of the pioneering Tuatara Beer Brewery which they use to draw inspiration from. They produce small batch seasonal gins using a copper plate fractionating column still and pure rainwater captured on the property, and source many of their ingredients locally from family owned operations and backyard gardeners.

ISLAND GIN DISTILLERY, GREAT BARRIER ISLAND
islandgin.com

Secreted away on the remote but beautiful Great Barrier Island, Island Gin has a sustainable ethos towards producing their small batch gins. Their bottles are designed to reflect a Kina shell and are made with almost 50% reclaimed glass, meaning that just like no two kina shells are alike neither are their bottles. All of their gins are distilled in small batches using a copper still before heading to their solar-powered bottling line.

JUNIPER DISTILLERY, RANGIORA
juniperdistillery.com

Seated in the vibrant country town of Rangiora to the north of Christchurch, Juniper Distillery is a garage-based micro-distillery that produces small runs of gin and gin liqueurs using a 50L pot still. They use a sugar wash fermentation as the base to make their spirits which are all hand-bottled, labelled, and sealed with wax.

KAIMAI BREWING & DISTILLING CO., WAIKINO
kaimaibrewinganddistilling.co.nz

Based at the historic Waikino Hotel in the Coromandel's beautiful Karangahake Gorge, Kaimai Brewing & Distilling Co. hand craft single batch gins. Inspired by old stories of the gold mining era, they celebrate the heritage of the land as well as the people and history of the gorge and surrounding areas.

KĀKĀPŌ DISTILLERY, WHANGAPARĀOA
kakapodistillery.co.nz

Anchored on the scenic Whangaparaoa Peninsula to the north of Auckland, Kakapo Distillery was founded on three key ideas: a love for Aotearoa, a passion for conservation, and a desire to make good gin. They use traditional methods with a copper alquitar to bring out Aotearoa's native forests and botanicals in their gins while being eco-conscious at every step and donating 10% of profits to the Kakapo Recovery fund.

KATIPŌ DISTILLING CO., NAPIER
katipodistilling.com

Housed somewhere in the New Zealand Art Deco capital of Napier, Katipo Distilling Co. was born around a campfire on Whirinaki Beach where the native spider that is their namesake was spotted crawling beside a glass of 'homebrew' gin. They make their gin using an alembic still and traditional botanicals along with Nelson Sauvin hops as their 'secret' herb and Kiwi innovation.

KIM CLIFFORD DISTILLERY, CROMWELL
kimclifford.co.nz

Located in idyllic Cromwell at the heart of Otago's fruit industry, Kim Clifford Distillery is centred on the ethos that life is for living and that friendships should be celebrated, sincerely and often. They craft their spirits to capture the essence of the people and places that inspire them for enjoyment in the company of great people.

KINGS LIQUOR, AUCKLAND
kingsliquor.co.nz

Huddled on the northern edge of Auckland in the suburb of Rosedale, Solace is produced by Kings Liquor which has been producing spirits since 1985. They produce small, handcrafted, artisanal batches of triple distilled gin which is echoed in their hand-illustrated labels that reflect the traditional crafting and blending of their recipes.

KIWI SPIRIT DISTILLERY, MOTUPIPI
kiwispiritdistillery.co.nz

Sheltered in the beautiful Golden Bay area of the Tasman region, Kiwi Spirit Distillery are a world away from the hustle and bustle of city life. Focusing on small batch distillation to deliver superior quality, they are committed to attention to detail and using all-natural ingredients to produce the best natural, preservative-free spirits. They endeavour to minimise their impact on the world by taking a sustainable approach to their craft.

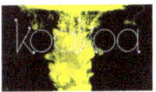

KOAKOA, PARAPARAUMU
koakoa.nz

Situated just a couple of minutes away from the Paraparaumu Beach shoreline on the spectacular Kapiti Coast, Koakoa, which means 'happiness' in Te Reo, distil both liqueurs and spirits. They use sustainable New Zealand ingredients and water filtered down from the Tararua ranges to make fine stuff, without the stuffiness, and give people what they want.

LADY H SPIRITS, AUCKLAND
ladyhspirits.com

Conceived in a garage in the depths of Central Otago and realised in Auckland, Lady H Spirits was started with the drive of creating a gin that would make the best Martini. They aim to show the world something a little different that can sing from its own song sheet.

LAMMERMOOR DISTILLERY, LAMMERMOOR
lammermoordistillery.com

Set amongst the tussock and wide open spaces of the Maniototo in Central Otago, Lammermoor Distillery sits at the heart of a 15,000 acre station with a connection to 1800s moonshining and built with materials sourced from the land around it. They use fresh spring water from the hills around them and grow their own grain, malt, mash, ferment, distil, and mature on site for their range of spirits which includes whisky and gin.

LAUGHING CLUB GIN, CHRISTCHURCH
laughingclubgin.com

Secreted away in the urban sprawl of Christchurch, Laughing Club gin takes inspiration from the roaring 20s, luxury Raffles Hotel in Singapore, and a legend about a raucous club by the same name. They use traditional methods with copper pot stills to triple distil their small batch gins which are made using pure New Zealand artesian water.

LAVENDER HILL, RIVERHEAD
lavenderhill.co.nz

Secluded on the outskirts of the historic township of Riverhead to the north of Auckland, Lavender Hill operates from a small working farm. Their central philosophy is to create products with a connection to the land and superb provenance, using handcrafted and sustainable ingredients to achieve this.

LIGHTHOUSE DISTILLERY, MARTINBOROUGH
lighthousegin.co.nz

Located in the warm micro-climate of Martinborough in the Wairarapa that supports a thriving local agriculture and viticulture, Lighthouse is one of New Zealand's oldest craft gins. Taking inspiration from the region's iconic Cape Palliser Lighthouse and its association with craftsmanship they only use the purest water filtered from high in the nearby Remutaka Ranges in their twice distilled gins.

LIMITED LABEL, QUEENSTOWN
ltdlabel.com

Sequestered away somewhere in beautiful Queenstown beneath the Southern Alps, Limited Label is a brand with the creative spirit at their heart, believing in art for the artist's sake, and making their gin for those who let their inner creative roam free. They contract a distiller in Marlborough to make their gin and each issue has a bottle with a different artist's work on it who receives 10% of the sale to foster the growth of their craft and the art community.

LONGSHOT DISTILLERY, ROLLESTON
longshotdistillery.co.nz

Tucked away in the thriving town of Rolleston just to the southwest of Christchurch, LongShot Distillery is a family-run micro-distillery that partly takes its name from their surname, Long. They have a love for gin and passion for craft distilling, which they pour into their range of gins call The Racketeer.

LYTTELTON DISTILLERY COMPANY, LYTTELTON
lytteltondistillery.co.nz

Nestled in the colourful port town of Lyttelton beneath the undulating Port Hills, Lyttelton Distillery Company was born out of a discussion with friends during a Labour Weekend that quickly turned into a focus on gin once things got started.

They make their spirits using their own base alcohol and a range of New Zealand sourced botanicals with an approach that is influenced by the traditions of gin-making and reflects aspects of the contemporary.

MT. FYFFE DISTILLERY, KAIKŌURA
mtfyffedistillery.co.nz

Arrayed amongst the foothills of Mt Fyffe near stunning Kaikoura, Mt. Fyffe Distillery forage many of their botanicals from around their own sheep farm on the slopes and the local area. They use a Portuguese 40L copper alembic still to craft small batches with their own spring water which are bottled and labelled by hand.

THE NATIONAL DISTILLERY COMPANY, NAPIER
nationaldistillery.nz

Ensconced in the commercial-industrial northern waterfront of Napier, The National Distillery Company resides in one of the cities architectural crown jewels. Built in 1931 following the Napier earthquake, it reflects the influences of Art Nouveau and Modernism, or Art Deco, which were in vogue at the time. They blend modern distilling techniques with time-honoured traditions, looking to this duality to inspire their creativity and overall approach to gin making.

NO8 DISTILLERY, DUNEDIN
no8distillery.com

Tucked into the Dog with Two Tails café and bar in the outer ring of Dunedin's Octagon, No8 Distillery take their name from the mentality and saying that arose from fixing anything with a piece of number 8 wire. This carries through into their experimental and unconventional approach to extraction and reconfigurable Franken-still named "Therese".

PAPAITI GIN, ŪPOKONGARO
papaitigin.co.nz

Based in the small village of Upokongaro on the banks of the Whanganui River just to the north of Whanganui itself, Papaiti Gin is the answer that came about after a couple moved into a new house and had the question of what to do with the fruit from two sizeable pear orchards. They locally source as many botanicals as possible, many of which grow on their property, to make their gin.

PAPAKA ROAD DISTILLERY, NGUNGURU
papakaroad.co.nz

Anchored on the bank of the Ngunguru River in the stunning Tutukaka Coast, Papaka Road Distillery aim to create product that is unique to their slice of Northland. They are focused on creating a signature taste using natural botanicals and fresh, locally sourced produce along with water from the pristine river catchment.

PINK & WHITE GEOTHERMAL GIN, ROTORUA
pinkandwhite.co.nz

Surrounded by the geothermal wonders of Rotorua, Pink & White Geothermal Gin take their name from the famed terraces that were lost in the 1886 eruption of Mount Tarawera and town's history of hospitality. Their vision is to build a distillery that utilises 100% renewable geothermal energy through a boiler to produce the most sustainable spirit.

POLLEN GIN, NELSON
pollengin.nz

Located in the relaxed southern Nelson suburb of Stoke, Pollen Gin came about after a spring spent in London plagued by hay fever until it was relieved by a few gin and tonics. They craft their gin using Canadian pure grain alcohol, natural New Zealand artesian water from beneath their distillery, and a blend of organic, home-grown, and handpicked botanicals giving it a low histamine content.

PREMIUM LIQUOR CO., AUCKLAND
premiumliquor.co.nz

Set amongst the sprawl and variety of Auckland city, Premium Liquor Co. produce a wide range of alcohols and mixers. They hand craft and triple distil their Rose & Twig gins in small batches, each with five different botanicals, to make each one unique and emphasise the beauty in being different.

REEFTON DISTILLING CO., REEFTON
reeftondistillingco.com

Stationed in the West Coast town of Reefton deep in the Inangahua River Valley, Reefton Distilling Co. is a modern distillery in an age old town that names their gin in honour of the local legend Bridget 'Biddy' Goodwin, a pipe-smoking, gin-toting, 4-foot-tall gold prospector who lived in the 1800s. They use large numbers of native botanicals from the surrounding rainforest to achieve a distinct West Coast flavour in their spirits.

REID + REID DISTILLERY, MARTINBOROUGH
reidandreid.co.nz

Based in the warm micro-climate of Martinborough in the Wairarapa that supports a thriving local agriculture and viticulture, Reid + Reid was founded in 2015 by two brothers with backgrounds in engineering and beverage production. They seek to challenge the perception of a 'classic' gin and promote New Zealand's unique native flora.

RIOT & ROSE SPIRITS, BLENHEIM
riotandrose.com

Established in Blenheim at the heart of the Marlborough wine region, Riot & Rose is one of only a handful of distilleries in New Zealand that are female owned and operated. Forefronting this in their brand and ethos, they aim to create contemporary gins that allow you to reflect your own style. This is emphasised by the way that their gins are based on different time periods which were poignant in gin history.

RUIN DISTILLERY, UPPER HUTT
ruindistillery.co.nz

Perched on the side of the quiet Moonshine Valley next to Upper Hutt, Ruin Distillery takes its name from the old gin moniker 'mother's ruin' in a wry nod and as a challenge to rise up. Possibly one of the world's smallest commercial distilleries at only 4m2, they combine 30 years of home distilling experience and a six plate flute still to produce small batches in individually numbered bottles.

SANDYMOUNT DISTILLERY, OTAGO PENINSULA
sandymount.nz

Cloaked by the hills of the Otago Peninsula beneath Pukehiki and Larnach Castle, Sandymount Distillery is fed by spring water from below their farm and surrounded by abundant native flora. They take inspiration from the beautiful landscape around them and its history in creating their handcrafted, small batches.

SCAPEGRACE DISTILLING CO., BENDIGO
scapegracedistillery.com

Tucked away on the hillside above Lake Dunstan, Scapegrace makes their gin using glacial water that takes 80 years to filter through the rock of the Southern Alps before being released into an aquifer. They use a restored 19th century hand-beaten copper pot still to create their gins in the same way it was done back then. This is reflected in their bottles which are a modern take on the genever bottles from 200 years ago.

SIMPLY PURE, TE PUNA
simplypure.co.nz

Sequestered away between the Kaimai Ranges and Tauranga, Simply Pure was born of the desire to create premium spirits for the global market that are quintessentially New Zealand. They distil their gin five times in a copper reflux still using organic botanicals whenever possible, which is inspired by and named for the very rare and endangered Chatham Island's Black Robin, and donate to ecological and environmental charities for every bottle sold.

SIR WINSTON GIN, AUCKLAND
sirwinstongin.com

Nestled in the bustling industrial area of Auckland's East Tamaki, Sir Winston Gin is a collaboration between 1919 Distilling and The Churchill Auckland to create a brand that emulates the eponymous statesman's class and sophistication. They use a range of botanicals to make their gin including Lapsang tea, which was a particular favourite of Churchill's.

THE SPIRITS WORKSHOP, CHRISTCHURCH
thespiritsworkshop.co.nz

Established in the light industrial area of Christchurch's suburb Sydenham, The Spirits Workshop set out from the start to create truly unique and individual gins that stand out from the crowd and the tonic. To hold true to these values their gins are made "grain to glass" where possible, in small batches using their copper pot still.

STORM BLACK WOLF GIN, AUCKLAND
blackwolfgin.co.nz

Standing amongst the urban sprawl of Auckland city, Storm Black Wolf Gin has spun out of the women's clothing brand

Storm and the belief that their customers might also like a good gin, choosing the wolf for its symbolism as a matriarch and one that resonates with what their designs represent. They work with The National Distillery Company in Napier to make their gin, focusing on the infusion of lemon and lime.

STRANGE NATURE DISTILLING, MARLBOROUGH
strangenaturegin.com

Stationed in the heart of the Marlborough wine region, Strange Nature Distilling was born out of a lifetime's winemaking and the exploration of new possibilities. They use alcohol removed from sustainable grown New Zealand Sauvignon Blanc wine as the base for their gin which is then distilled with just juniper to allow the flavours of its origins to come through.

TAUPŌ DISTILLING CO., TAUPŌ
taupodistilling.com

Positioned in scenic Taupo and surrounded by diverse landscapes, Taupo Distilling Co. is a home-based distillery that came about from long summer afternoons drinking G&Ts at 5 Mile Bay. They make their gin in small 50L batches with New Zealand produced botanicals wherever possible using a combination of maceration and vapour infusion which is cut with water from Mount Ruapehu.

THOMSON WHISKY DISTILLERY, RIVERHEAD
thomsonwhisky.com

Based in the historic township of Riverhead to the north of Auckland, Victor Gin was born out of tinkering and experimentation at the Thomson Whisky Distillery. Taking inspiration from the world of music they focus on fresh botanicals and the heavy use of juniper to create the best spirits they can.

TWELFTH HOUR DISTILLERY, AUCKLAND
twelfthhourdistillery.co.nz

Ringed by the vibrant communities of South Auckland, Twelfth Hour Distillery was born from a small group of friends' desire to fuse fresh, exotic botanicals from around the globe with New Zealand made gin. They hand craft small batches, spending many nights working well past midnight, which is the origin of their name.

THE VICAR'S SON, AUCKLAND
vicarsson.co.nz

Produced in the heart of Point Chevalier in Auckland with a zero waste policy, The Vicar's Son is the smallest commercial distiller in the world. Operating a 6L finishing still that produces a max of nine bottles per batch, they don't use any filtering techniques so that what you see and taste is as it came out of the still.

WAIHEKE DISTILLING CO., WAIHEKE ISLAND
waihekedistilling.co.nz

Enveloped by bush and former pasture land on the eastern end of Waiheke Island, Waiheke Distilling Co. have developed a large garden that exemplifies the botanical story of their spirits. Overlooking Cowes Bay, with its history of hospitality and leisure, they focus on crafting botanical spirits in a sustainable and meaningful way.

WAITOKI WASHHOUSE DISTILLERY, WAITOKI
washhousedistillery.co.nz

Secluded amongst the many dairy farms that surround the small town of Waitoki to the north of Auckland, Waitoki Washhouse Distillery distils small batches in a handmade copper alembic still from Portugal it what was once a home garage. They pride themselves on the very manual nature of their process and lack of pretences.

THE WHITE SHEEP CO., WHANGAMATĀ
thewhitesheepco.com

Located in the popular beach town of Whangamata which borders The Coromandel Forest Park, The White Sheep Co. is a boutique distillery that handcrafts a range of spirits and liqueurs using premium New Zealand sheep's milk. The milk takes two weeks to ferment using special yeasts and is then distilled into a full strength spirit using a traditional style copper still to retain some of the sheep milk's flavours.

WILD DIAMOND DISTILLERY, QUEENSTOWN
wilddiamond.co.nz

Resting on the Kelvin Peninsula overlooking Lake Wakatipu and Queenstown, Wild Diamond takes its name from the natural elements that surround them. They select their botanicals based on their quality and character, sourcing them both internationally and locally. Maintaining their connection to their environment, their stills are powered by renewable wind and water energy, and invest back into water and aquatic habitat enhancement, recovery, and restoration.

YEN GIN, CHRISTCHURCH
yen.co.nz

Situated somewhere in the hubbub of Christchurch, Yen Gin is named for a concept of intense desire that they take as a drive to seek out the things that inspire them, which in their case are the possibilities of gin. They aim to challenge the confines of traditional branding and flavour with their gin which is also the first NFT tokenised gin brand in the world.

www.ingramcontent.com/pod-product-compliance
Lightning Source LLC
Chambersburg PA
CBHW062045290426
44109CB00027B/2740